THE CHAT GPT EDGE

UNLEASHING THE LIMITLESS POTENTIAL OF AI
USING SIMPLE AND CREATIVE PROMPTS TO BOOST
PRODUCTIVITY, MAXIMIZE EFFICIENCY, AND GROW
YOUR BUSINESS FAST

FLETCHER PARKS

CONTENTS

Introduction   7

Part I
CHATGPT 101

1. WHY EVERYONE'S OBSESSED WITH
   CHATGPT   15
   G-P-What?   17
   How ChatGPT Works   23
   ChatGPT's Ten Basic Abilities   26

2. AI IN EVERYDAY LIFE   33
   10 Ways AI Is Already Improving
   Your Life   34

3. SETTING UP CHATGPT FOR YOUR
   BUSINESS: STEP-BY-STEP GUIDE   41
   Starting to Use ChatGPT   42
   Cool Things to Try With ChatGPT   44

Part II
HOW TO CREATE YOUR NEW AI
VIRTUAL ASSISTANT

4. THE "BUSINESS BRAIN" METHOD FOR
   TRAINING CHATGPT   51
   The "Business Brain" Method   52
   Learning to Speak to ChatGPT   56
   What You Can Do With This Method   58
   Bonus: Non-Native Features and
   Extensions   64

5. FROM CHATGPT TO BUSINESS BRAIN   69
How to Use the Business Brain Method
With ChatGPT   70
Practice   83

Part III
USING CHATGPT TO SUPERCHARGE
YOUR LIFE

6. BOOSTING BUSINESS PRODUCTIVITY
AND EFFICIENCY   91
Our Imaginary Business   92
Marketing and Sales   95
Customer Service   107
Human Resources and Recruitment   115
Accounting and Finance   123
Considerations   130

7. ENHANCING YOUR PERSONAL LIFE   133
Dating and Relationship Advice   135
Improve Your Writing   136
Helping With Studies   137
Create Diet Plans and Recipes   139
Finding Ways to Make Money   141

Part IV
ENVISIONING THE FUTURE

8. LATEST DEVELOPMENTS IN
CHATBOT TECHNOLOGY   145
How ChatGPT Is Impacting the Future
of AI   147
ChatGPT Integration With Other
Platforms   150
Promising Investments in the AI Race   152

9. WILL AI REPLACE HUMANS?   161

   Why AI Can't Replace Humans
   —For Now   165

   The Rise of Generative AI   168

   Final Considerations   177

   Conclusion   181

   References   185

INTRODUCTION

Artificial intelligence will reach human levels by around 2029. Follow that out further to, say, 2045, and we will have multiplied the intelligence – the human biological machine intelligence of our civilization – a billion-fold.

— RAY KURZWEIL, AMERICAN
INVENTOR AND FUTURIST

ChatGPT is the "new cool kid on the block." Everyone is talking about it and some people are even using it to replace it as a web search engine—although this is not what it was created for. While Google uses algorithms to rank and find billions of pages on the internet, ChatGPT does not have the same ability or the same features to replace the search engine (Shukla, 2023). But this does not mean that the tool is unuseful—far from this. ChatGPT provides its users with a more conversational-like approach, making it easier to understand some subjects.

But even though ChatGPT is the new "sensation" on the market, it is far from being a novelty or the best artificial intelligence (AI) tool that can be used. For you to have an idea, companies such as Google, Meta, and others known as Big Tech, already had their own AI programs, but they either had limited use or were restricted to the public. While these companies were more cautious, Microsoft's OpenAI, owner of ChatGPT, can be credited for its "boldness in releasing the tool to the public and some boldness in allowing the bot to address some, but not all, controversial subjects" (Elgan, 2023).

These companies are now running against time to ensure that they place in the market tools that can outperform ChatGPT. Because of this, it is likely that we will become more familiar with previously tech-exclusive words such as "prompting the program." But don't worry, I wouldn't think about writing this book if it wasn't to teach you everything there is to know about using ChatGPT—especially if it is used to help grow your business.

If you enter LinkedIn today, it is likely you will find all sorts of information regarding the AI platform. You will see people saying good things, others saying bad. You will see some people talking about building businesses by using it and others that claim they are killing their jobs. Everybody seems to have an opinion. My point of view? ChatGPT can be an incredibly useful tool in helping you design and grow your business, but we must never forget the importance played by "the human factor." I wouldn't be writing this book if I at least didn't consider this possibility.

Nevertheless, companies are becoming more reliant on it—real estate companies are using AI to generate their listings and Buzzfeed is using ChatGPT to create news for their website (Elgan, 2023 and Sharma, 2023). And if you think that these are the only places, you will be astounded to find out it is not. In a survey conducted with 1,000 managers, 48% claim that employees have been replaced by ChatGPT (Shukla, 2023). What is worse, the same poll indicated that 33% of their workforce will certainly be dismissed in exchange for the tool and 26% might. This number is even more alarming if you consider the prospect of what will happen in two years, 2025, when "63% of business leaders say ChatGPT will 'definitely' (32%) or 'probably' (31%) lead to workers being laid off" (Shukla, 2023).

But not all is gray in the future. As many things are new, we must be cautious. There is still a lot about the software that is unknown and that remains to be discovered. For example, one of the things you will see in this book is that there are several "hidden" features that few people know about. In addition to this, it is not as updated as many people may think. At the time this book was written in April 2023, ChatGPT informed its users that it contained reliable information up to September 2021 and that new updates would be limited.

This means that if you are going to use ChatGPT, you must check your sources and be sure that the information is updated. During my several tests with the tool, I asked for sources to the information it was giving me and the web pages did not exist. Does this make it a reliable tool to write papers? No. Will it substitute going to the doctor to learn more about your health? Definitely not. But can it help you become more productive and help you set up a new business? Most certainly.

And this is why this book will help you. Not only will you learn the most important things there are to learn about ChatGPT, but it will also help you supercharge your life. You will learn how to ask the right questions, find information that will help your productivity, and efficiently boost your business without the need of (much) consultancy. ChatGPT will be able to give you this. It is safe to say that if companies think that it is a good tool to help in their business, it can also be something positive for yours.

Get ready to jump into the Business Brain Method and see the benefits of leveraging ChatGPT to enhance your business and become a better professional. Are you ready? Let's go!

PART I

CHATGPT 101

1

WHY EVERYONE'S OBSESSED WITH CHATGPT

It was in late 2022 when the "boom" began. Companies were talking about it, students started using it, and the market was buzzing about this new artificial intelligence (AI) tool that had been released to the market. The impact was so big that it reached the mark of one million users just 5 days after it was released and, from there, the number only grew (Vanian, 2022). In only 2 months after its release, in early 2023, the application had already reached 100 million users (Gal, 2023). The success of the Microsoft-backed tool gained the market and while some were enthusiastic about it, others were worried.

The tech industry was worried about hackers using the program to create more powerful malicious code.

Teachers had to develop new abilities to identify papers that were written by the AI tool. Employees started fearing their jobs might be replaced by the tool. The ease that ChatGPT provided the user by mimicking conversations and providing answers to the most varied questions took the market by storm. The vast amount of information and the easy interaction had some people changing from search engines to the answers provided by the application, even though they were not always true, or accurate.

It did not matter that the page had a disclaimer saying that the information was only accurate to a certain date. Neither were users worried that it might provide incorrect information or that the instructions it provided could be harmful or biased—all of which are visibly exposed in the software's first page for the user to see. What is even worse, companies, of which most notably was the Korean electronic manufacturer Samsung, were pasting corporate proprietary information into the system without considering that this information would be stored and used to train the AI in the future, as it states in the tool's user guide.

There was still the data privacy issue. "OpenAI, the company behind ChatGPT, fed the tool some 300 billion words systematically scraped from the internet:

books, articles, websites and posts – including personal information obtained without consent" (Gal, 2023). Could your data have been there? Who knows? It could be, but we will never know. For some authors, the problem was even worse, since the program could replicate word by word the information that was contained in copyrighted books and articles. Cyber and data security personnel worldwide were alarmed with what they were seeing, and not without reason.

But what is ChatGPT? How does this tool work and how was the model developed? In this chapter, we are going to take a deeper look into the workings of the application and understand the technology used behind its development and how the tool works in general. In addition to this, I am going to give you an overview of its main abilities before we take a look into how it can effectively help you and your business. The first step will be understanding what this application is and an explanation into the technology used behind it. Are you ready?

G-P-WHAT?

We all know what "Chat" is, but what about the "GPT?" Are these just three meaningless letters taken from the mind of its creator or does it mean something? Well, GPT actually stands for **Generative Pre-Trained**

Transformer. Big word, right? But it is, in fact, a rather simple concept. I mean that this is an application that has been fed information, or been trained, to generate other data. For you to have an idea, ChatGPT was built with over 175 **billion** parameters, which makes it one of the most complex and complete applications to ever exist (Entrepreneur, 2023). As for the transformation part, it means that the information is processed and transformed based on the information that it is given, in this case, a sequence of words or letters.

In simple terms, we can say that ChatGPT is a software that will transform the data that it was previously trained with based on the information that is asked, or **prompted**, by the user. This is the reason why, for example, it is so important to pay attention to the small disclaimer that is placed in the opening page, where it says that the information might not be accurate after September 2021. This is because the data that was fed to the neural network was all previous to this date and, therefore, it might not have "knowledge" about the events after it for the simple reason that this information was not uploaded to the database.

But let's stop for a moment and look at a term that I have just used with which you might not be familiar: neural networks. While you might immediately associate the name with the neurons we have in our body, I can say that this is partially correct. A neural network in technology means that this is a computer system that learns and works like a human brain. "Just as the brain has pathways where information is stored and functions are carried out, AI uses neural networks to mimic that process to problem-solve, learn patterns and collect data" (Entrepreneur, 2023). These neural networks are the base of AI and, such as is the case of ChatGPT, it was trained by using natural language processing (NLP) which means that it was designed to interact and mimic a human conversation.

For this reason, when you prompt ChatGPT for information, it can come back with responses that will be similar to a conversation with another human. As we look deeper into the application in the last section of this chapter, you will see that it can react language-wise, just as a human would do, the reason for which some people are calling it a high-efficiency chatbot. However, different from the previous automatic systems that were commonly used, it has an extreme capability of carrying out conversations as humans would by generating responses instead of using pre-prepared answers. And this is a **major** game changer.

One of the motives is that because of this ability, it is able to replace humans in certain activities. For example, imagine a situation in which a person enters a business's website and prompts the online chat to obtain answers to their questions. You have probably experienced this and it came to a point where you just gave up because the answer was simply not satisfactory enough. In this case, the answers were too standard to help with more complex situations, but not as costly as having a human being employed to do so.

However, with ChatGPT, since it is able to reproduce and replicate human responses, a middle ground might just have been found. The tool will be able to answer questions based on the information it has stored in its system and generate responses based on each person's needs thus replacing the traditional chatbots as we know it and discarding the need of having a human carry out the job. Think of it: *How many jobs can you imagine would be replaced by automated tools simply because they can mimic human language?*

Although there is not much of a consensus among professionals on the number, specialists evaluate that 25% of all the existing jobs in the world could be replaced (Jones, 2023). Jones still informs that according to a Goldman Sachs study,

> AI could automate 25% of the entire labor market but can automate 46% of tasks in administrative jobs, 44% of legal jobs, and 37% of

architecture and engineering professions. Of course, AI is the least threatening to labor-intensive careers like construction (6%), installation and repair (4%), and maintenance (1%) (para. 3).

On the other hand, this might mean that companies would be able to save money in several areas. This is also related to one of the specific advantages that tools like ChatGPT have, the ability to learn. This means that because it is based on neural networks, the program will be able to learn according to the interactions that it has, making it more enhanced by the number of times it is used and the different prompts that it is given. This will increase its reach and, as its database is fed with more information and users provide feedback, improvements will be made.

Pretty cool right? But despite these awesome features that it has, it also has a few disadvantages. One of them is that the program is not completely free of bias, since it will determine the answer to the questions based on the information that it was previously given. In this sense, it will very much rationalize like a human. Suppose that you have been given the same information throughout your life and have developed bias on a certain subject. This means that whenever the subject is approached, you will use the knowledge you have to communicate. The same happens with ChatGPT. The information that it contains might not be 100% reliable because of its quality and the bias that was contained in the dataset that was used to train it (Administrator, 2023).

One example of this behavior was shown by Vanian (2022), who wrote that "ChatGPT produced song lyrics that implied women who wear lab coats are 'probably just there to clean the floor,' whereas men wearing lab coats 'probably got the knowledge and skills you're looking for.'" This means that if you are now using ChatGPT as a search engine, it might be time to rethink this attitude—at least for now.

While some of the answers can be right on target, others might be misleading and fake, which can mean bringing you harm if the "traditional" research methods are not carried out. Think about the example I have given you. When you ask ChatGPT something, it will give you an answer based on the information it has. It does not have the ability to search the internet for content or additional input, making it unreliable for current issues since there is always the possibility of error. It is similar to you studying plants for an exam in school when the content is about animals. While you might be able to input some ideas, you simply did not acquire this knowledge and, therefore, you will make mistakes on your test.

I can imagine that some wheels are turning inside your head and you are thinking that this might be too complex. I can assure you it is not as it seems. The process is relatively simple to understand some more of how ChatGPT works and the process through which the information goes when the software is being trained. I have separated a step-by-step process that will enable you to see the bigger picture. Read on to find out the inner workings of ChatGPT and learn how you can train it (with security precautions, of course).

HOW CHATGPT WORKS

Now, there is no one better to explain the inner workings of the ChatGPT functions than OpenAI themselves, so I am going to explain this to you based on a document that's published on their website. According to the company, the first thing that is done to prepare the application is to collect the data that they want to be trained upon and create specific rules that will apply to them (Lowe & Leike, 2022). Next, they get any information from this dataset that was fed to the AI and ask for a prompt, a question, to which they already know the answer to.

However, instead of waiting for the program to answer it, they apply a "label," meaning that they demonstrate to the application what is the expected behavior for this specific question. Therefore, they are teaching the model to the way they want it to think and react to this specific prompt. Once it has the expected answer, or output, the scientists will fine-tune ChatGPT with the learning parameters that they have established. This process is known as training the model under supervision.

I understand that it seems complex, so I am going to give you an example that will make it easier to understand. Suppose that you want to explain to a child what a tree is. You will then prompt ChatGPT with the following: *Explain what is a tree to a child*. The trainer will then tell the program that the correct answer would be to say that *a tree is a form of a plant that has a trunk and leaves*. Based on the answer that the trainer has given, ChatGPT will understand that this simple way is the correct way to answer what is a tree to a child.

Now, this is not all, there is yet another step, which is to collect different answers that can be applied to the first one, such as explaining why trees grow, explain photosynthesis, explain leaves, and so on. This is when several output models will be created and the labeler, or trainer, will **rank** these answers from best to worst so that the application can understand what is acceptable and what is not. For example, explaining photosynthesis to a child in detail might not make sense to them, but saying that a tree has leaves and that some of them have flowers and fruit can be a good alternative. During this process, the trainer is literally giving feedback to the program so that it can understand, or learn, the best way to answer the question of what is a tree when speaking to a child. Once these answers are obtained, the model will be then once again trained so that it can identify the best reward.

After this is done, the last part includes creating a policy that will reward the model and use what is called reinforcement learning. This means that if you see an explanation and give it "one star" quality, it will be a bad answer and the user will be dissatisfied. On the other hand, if ChatGPT asks you the quality of the answer and you give it "five stars" you will be rewarded for doing a good job. Based on these evaluations, it will **reinforce** answers that are positive and well ranked and will **discard** those answers that are not considered good enough.

During the training process, this is done by prompting the application with a different input and evaluating the quality of the output it will generate. Then, the same process that you have seen before will be applied: the trainer will calculate a reward for the output. If it is positive, then this will reinforce the learning process because the answer that was given was good. In this case, the process will continue and the machine will see a reinforcement in the technique that it is currently using. This whole process is known as **reinforcement learning from human feedback** (RLHF), since the program needs the input of a person to tell them what is a suitable answer and what is not.

Now, we know **how** ChatCPT does it, but **what** exactly is it able to do? Worry not! We are going to look at it now. As you will see, ChatGPT has ten basic abilities that makes it the powerful tool that it is. Read on to find out what they are and some of its advantages.

CHATGPT'S TEN BASIC ABILITIES

When you think about ChatGPT, you must know that it is more than a text generator. It is also capable of coding and analyzing code, resolving mathematical problems (although limited capacity), and much, much more. In addition to this, if you know how to code in Python, it is possible to embed some of your personalized code to give it specific commands, including creating images! Even if you are not a coder, there are still many things it can do, as we will now see.

- **Automated text generation:** This is the main tool for which ChatGPT is known for—

creating text. You can ask it to write a story, prompt it for information on a certain subject, and even write an e-mail or an ad campaign for you and your business. What is even better is that all this will be done using a language structure similar to the way we speak, making it much easier to adapt and personalize.

- **Personalized text generation:** Speaking of personalization, there is a feature in ChatGPT called **fine tuning**. This means that you can train it to, for example, write a text as you would. However, to do this, you must first "feed" it the information such as samples of your work or texts that you would like it to mimic. Once this is done, you can tell it to write about anything using the information that you had previously given it. An important reminder here, once again, is that this information will be stored in its databases for further consultation. Therefore, if we are talking about something that is copyrighted or proprietary, you might want to be careful about adding it.

- **Summarize text:** Suppose that you want to know more about a short book that has your interest. One of the things you can do is ask ChatGPT to summarize it for you. If the information that you want is in the database (remember, up to September 2021), it is likely that it will bring you a summary with the main points of the book, study, report, or news article that you have selected, making it all much easier to understand the information that might be too technical. Keep in mind, however, that ChatGPT has a limited capacity and while it is unlikely that it will summarize longer novels, you might have success in doing the same for shorter texts.

- **Text translation:** One of the other major features of ChatGPT is that it is able to translate text quickly and efficiently. According to OpenAI, the application currently supports 98 languages that can be translated from and, guess what, even provide speech-to-text features (OpenAI, n.d.). However, while the translation tool will not need any coding, if you want to perform a speech-to-text action you will need to use coding, since the program still does not recognize using a microphone and, thus, uploading the file to the program would be needed. Still according to OpenAI (n.d.), for these services "we only list the languages that exceeded <50% word error rate (WER) which is an industry standard benchmark for speech to text model accuracy. The model will return results for languages not listed above but the quality will be low."

- **Explain and write code:** If you are a beginner at coding, or even an experienced developer who is having difficulty in understanding a certain code, ChatGPT can help you with this! The program is able to write and explain code in different programming languages. Another awesome feature is that it can also help you debug code that might give you problems and you cannot understand why it is not working. You might even be able to prompt it to tell you the process of how to add the code to the application itself so that you can carry out the actions that you need it to perform.

- **Completing texts:** If you prompt ChatGPT with the beginning of a text, it will use the information contained in its database to complete the text. Nevertheless, since we are still talking about an AI tool and not a crystal ball, it might bring you the output that you are expecting. This might mean that if you ask something like: The sea is... and ask it to complete, you can have varied outputs that range from technical and scientific information about the sea to answers as simple as "the sea is blue." This will depend on how you ask the question and how specific you are. Just as we will see in the next item, **answering questions**, it is important that you know how to correctly prompt ChatGPT so that it understands what you want and the level of detail that you need.

- **Answering questions:** Now, this feature is one of the most awesome that ChatGPT has and is the reason why I mentioned earlier that some people are replacing search engines for the application. This is because based on the data that it has, the program can answer almost any question with an alarming precision. And what is better, you can have it answered in the format that you prefer: numbered lists, bullet points, essay form, you name it. On the other hand, once again I must remind you that there might be some bias and some incorrect information because of the database from which it obtains its information. Therefore, while it can be really useful, it is important to always double-check the information to make sure that it is correct.

- **Name recognition:** If you ask ChatGPT who Steve Jobs was, it will answer you. If you ask them about a recognized company, it will do the same. In addition to this, even if you ask it about a specific location, it might be able to give you information on that place. This is because the application can recognize names and locations with data that exists until the date to which it has been updated. This means that if you ask for the population of a specific country, it will be based on 2021 data, as well as it might not recognize new companies (well, except for itself) that have not been entered in the database after the stipulated date.

- **Understand feelings:** Remember when I mentioned that ChatGPT uses NLP to make its answers similar to the way humans speak. This means that it is also capable of understanding the feeling of what is being said based on the analysis of some keywords. This means that you can ask it to write you a text that contains emotions, for example, or even structure the text to have it convey the intent that you desire. This can be a useful tool in marketing, for example to determine how to structure the texts of certain ads or analyze the public perception of something that you have created.

- **Aid with grammar:** If you left school a while ago and can't remember what are adverbs, prepositions, and all those other parts of speech that we learned in class, then ChatGPT is here to save you. No more struggling to help your children understand their English homework because you can use the application to help you figure it out. If you prompt it with a sentence, for example, you can ask it to identify what parts of speech each word belongs to and even help you structure your sentences better so that they are more understandable.

2

AI IN EVERYDAY LIFE

By now, you are probably excited to find out first-hand what you can make ChatGPT do. But the application is far from being the first AI tool that is available in the market. From the Siris, Alexas, or Google Assistant, to the auto complete that is available in your phone texting app, many things we use today have AI and we might not even realize it. In order to fully comprehend what ChatGPT's capable of, let's take a look at the various ways that most of us are using AI on a daily basis, some of which might surprise you!

10 WAYS AI IS ALREADY IMPROVING YOUR LIFE

- **Voice assistants:** As I mentioned earlier, if you use any of the voice assistants available in the market, you are using AI and might not even know it. This is because the way that we interact with them, and the way that they understand what we are saying, is also using NLP, just like ChatGPT. For example, think about how you can record your grocery list to them or how they seem to be interconnected with your digital life. In addition to this, if you greet them "good morning," it is likely that they will answer you, as well as if you ask them to tell you a joke. By understanding, interacting, and replicating human speech, these tools enable us to help us with several tasks and keep our lives organized.

- **Food ordering services:** Have you ever noticed that when you open your food delivery application it seems to know exactly what you like? This is because most of these platforms use AI to store your preferences and later make suggestions based on your most common orders. This means that it will make a calculation based on the number of times you have requested certain food types and place them on top of the list because it is likely that you will order it again based on your behavior.

- **Navigation apps:** If you have ever used a navigation program to avoid traffic while going somewhere or coming back, you were using AI, did you know that? This is because these applications use AI to measure the number of people in a determined region (based usually on the number of devices in the area) and establish if there is significant traffic. In addition to this, it will analyze the information from other uses to determine alternate routes that can be used based on the time that they take to complete the full route.

- **Personalized marketing:** Let's say that you spent the morning searching the internet for the perfect gift for a friend and then go out for lunch. Later, when you came back you logged into your social media page and, what a surprise! All the ads that you see for sponsored products are related to the products you were searching. Well, let me tell you that this is not a coincidence, but rather AI working to determine what interests you. In this case, companies are using this technology to store your search history and preference to suggest you products in which you might be interested. This is the optimization of marketing tools that target a public with specific wants, needs, and demands, and that make it easier for companies to "target" their customers and have a higher probability of a purchase.

- **Social media:** Speaking of social media, how many times have you noticed that you seem to see only the updates of certain friends, while other friends do not show up at all? This is because AI is filtering out the content of those people with whom you interact the least and prioritizing showing you the information shared by those you interact with the most. Therefore, if you have a friend you might want to know more from or see more of the actions, a solution would be to interact with their publications. Another interesting thing is that AI will use different "weights" to determine what will be shown. For example, the rank of the person in your feed will depend on whether you like, comment, or share their content, which will also be the basis for showing content of similar individuals that are not necessarily in your network.

- **Autocorrect:** Friends to some, enemies to many, the autocorrect feature that we have on our electronic devices are a classic example of the work AI can do. While on one hand it will analyze what you are typing to suggest potential words based on the previous and the next letters, it can also work predicting what you will speak. If you have ever seen those social media challenges where they ask the user to start a sentence and let autocorrect finish it for you, this is AI working. It will complete the sentence for you based on your most commonly used words within that context, which is why sometimes we are able to have such a good laugh at what some people post.

- **Search engines:** A similar principle is used when you are using a search engine to look for something. When you start typing your query these platforms usually will help you fill in the rest of the sentence based on several items such as highest ranked questions and user history. This means that AI will make suggestions to complete your input based on the most likely phrase comparing it to other similar searches made by other users. In addition to this, if you search for a specific subject, you might notice that it will possibly fill in the remainder of the sentence with the subject that you have been searching, all the wonder of the data stored in its AI database.

- **Recommending products:** If you think about Amazon, Spotify, Netflix, and other service or streaming providers, you will notice one thing in common: They seem to know what you will be interested in purchasing, watching or listening to. This is because these platforms, much like the one for food delivery, work based on a tool that determines the behavior of its user. What this translates to is that if the user is accustomed to watching horror movies, it will recommend other products with the same characteristics based on how they interact with the platform as well as to what other users with the same behavior acted. This is why whether you are listening to music, watching a series, or buying something, it knows exactly what you will be interested in—AI will analyze the patterns, ratings, and possibilities to see what will be the best recommendation for you.

- **Facial recognition (Face ID on phones):** Many smartphones today have a resource in which the owner uses facial recognition to unlock the device. This happens because there is an embedded AI application in its software that enables the phone to recognize faces based on certain focal points of the face. When all of these characteristics are analyzed together, they give the software a "picture" composed of a set of data that will determine if this is the person or not. Due to this, some more primitive forms of the tool cannot identify the face if you are smiling or with your eyes wide open. Although this is not an issue in more modern programs, it still is not 100% effective and might have errors.

- **Banking:** One of the safest (and maybe most annoying) that AI presents can be seen when it is applied to banking. This is because these financial institutions use software based on AI to establish spending and transfer patterns to bring a higher security to the user. This means that if you have ever had a day in which you spent more than you usually do, you have probably received a notification from the bank asking you to confirm that it was you or that the transaction was denied. While this is good to prevent fraud and problems for the cases in which a security problem is true, it can also be tiresome if you just felt like you wanted to go on a shopping spree or spend a little more on that present for a friend.

3

SETTING UP CHATGPT FOR YOUR BUSINESS: STEP-BY-STEP GUIDE

W ith everything that you have read so far, you might be thinking, *Well, it all sounds very good and very nice, but will I be able to use this tool*? To answer your question, let me tell you that children are using ChatGPT to do their homework and write their essays (Duboust & Bello, 2023). Yes, you read this correctly. This topic is so "hot" in different communities that there is a whole debate on whether schools should allow AI to be used in completing homework. While students are excited that they have a tool that can mimic their writing to write the essays that have long been demanded from them for evaluation, teachers from all education levels are worried that this might hinder the learning process and the ways students are assessed.

For you to have an idea, as soon as people started using ChatGPT, the academic world started to panic. Because of all the "problems" that were generated and the fear of students cheating or plagiarizing, OpenAI and several other companies launched a special tool that enables professionals to determine if a specific content was created using AI tools. These tools, depending on the one you are using, will help establish if there are enough elements to determine that the content is AI generated or if it was created by a human.

But how does this apply to me? While you might not be writing school essays or doing homework, my intention here was to give you an example of how easy it can be to manage ChatGPT. As I will now show you, to start using the tool you don't need to know how to code or have any technological abilities. All that the application will ask of you is your email and a password to login and you are able to start using it. In addition to showing you how you will login, I will also provide you with some examples and practice exercises that will help you to test its ability and get you started being familiar with the tool.

STARTING TO USE CHATGPT

To start using ChatGPT, all you will need is a device that has a web browser connected to the internet. Once this is done, you must follow these seven steps.

1. Go to **chat.openai.com/auth/login**.
2. Press "sign up."
3. Enter your email or log in with one of the other possibilities, such as Google and Microsoft emails.
4. Enter a password of your preference.
5. Check your email and verify the provided email address.
6. Go to **chat.openai.com/chat** and sign in with your credentials.
7. Read the instructions and disclaimers available in the first page so you are aware of what to expect.

You can now start a chat by typing in a question or request in the text box at the bottom of the screen. This will be called **prompting** and is how you will interact with the tool. As you will soon see, it is possible to obtain the most varied information from all different topics. Remember the limitations I have spoken to you about and have fun trying it out!

COOL THINGS TO TRY WITH CHATGPT

Now that you have an account, you will be able to prompt ChatGPT to give you information, explain topics, and even make jokes. Try using it a little so that you can get used to the way it works before we move on to the next part of the book when we will start seeing how you can use ChatGPT as a business tool.

In the meantime, while you are exploring it, remember that the output that it will give you will depend on what and how you ask. Therefore, be sure that if you want specific information about something, that you write down the details in the prompt so that it can understand what it is that you want. On the list below, I will give you different examples of how to prompt the application, one generic and one more specific so you can see the differences. However, the output will not be provided because the answers may vary according to the user.

- **Make jokes**

  Can you tell me a joke?
  Can you tell me an elephant joke?
  Can you tell me a long elephant joke?

- **Explain complex topics**

Tell me what physics is.
Can you explain the concept of quantum physics?

- **Write essays**

Write me an essay about the history of the United States.
Write me a comprehensive and detailed essay about the history of the United States.
Write me a comprehensive, detailed, and original essay about the history of the United States.

- **Make music**

Write the lyrics to a song.
Write me the lyrics to a song about love.
Write me the lyrics to a song about love and suggest a rhythm.

- **Play games**

What games can you play?
Let's play hangman!
Can you help me with a crossword puzzle?

- **Solve math problems**

Give me an example of solving a math problem.
Can you give me a solved example of a linear
function?
What is the result of 5 squared plus 3 squared?

- **Write code**

Write a code in Java to print "Hello, World!"
Write the code for a simple racing game in
Python.
What is the difference between printing "Hello,
World!" in Java and in Python?

- **Ask for movie recommendations**

Can you recommend a movie?
Can you recommend a good horror movie?
Can you recommend to me a horror movie that
was an Oscar winner?

- **Brainstorm ideas**

What is a good plot for a crime story?
Can you tell me the plot for a story about a criminal seeking justice?

Can you give me backstory ideas for a character that was a criminal?

- **Ask for a recipe**

Give me the recipe for chocolate chip cookies.
I have ham, eggs, and tomatoes in my fridge.
What can I cook for dinner?
Give me ideas and recipes for dishes that I can make for a romantic dinner.

I encourage you to try some of these for yourself and even make up some ideas regarding themes that you might find interesting. Try prompting ChatGPT to help you with grammar and sentence structure, to create a story, and much more. Once you are done exploring the tool, come back to the next part of this book, because it is time to get down to business!

In the next section, I will introduce you to the Business Brain Method and how you can use ChatGPT to help you grow your business or even start one from scratch. We will look at its applications for several different areas for the company such as hiring models, customer service, and marketing. In addition to this, I will help you learn how to adjust ChatGPT to "speak your language," by teaching how to fine-tune it to your needs and required specifications.

PART II

HOW TO CREATE YOUR NEW AI VIRTUAL ASSISTANT

THE "BUSINESS BRAIN" METHOD FOR TRAINING CHATGPT

I assume that you have, by now, become familiar with ChatGPT and that you have "played" with it some. Good for you! It is essential that you know how to work the application in order to get the best possible results. However, we are down to business now and I am going to teach you how you can make ChatGPT become your personal assistant and help it boost your business or start it from scratch.

The main thing that you have to know here is that, although many people use ChatGPT to perform certain activities, few of them really **understand** how to make it work in their favor. This might be because they are simply missing the key steps to do so, and I don't want this to happen to you. Therefore, this is what this chapter will be all about. I am going to teach you the best techniques and methods to obtain the best results from the tool and make sure that you have the best possible outcome.

I call this method the "Business Brain" Method because you will be feeding ChatGPT relevant information about your business or the one that you want to create and use its help to come up with solutions. The method is comprised of three steps,

1. Feeding the brain
2. Teaching the brain
3. Unleashing the brain.

In addition to this, we are also going to look at how you can learn to "speak" ChatGPTs language and the advantages that you will obtain from it. Therefore, without further delay, let's begin our learning path.

THE "BUSINESS BRAIN" METHOD

This method is all about transforming ChatGPT into the thinking center of your business. When you do this, you will see that it will be able to generate more specific answers tailored to your needs and within your established requirements. The first step of the process, as you have seen, is to "feed the brain." Let's take a look at how this works.

Feeding the Brain

This is the first most important part of the process of using ChatGPT to help you. Even so, it is the step that most people miss and the reason why they usually get generic results rather than targeted actions on what to do. Think of it this way: When we, humans, want to talk about something, we must first **know** about the subject to discuss it with property. The same works for ChatGPT. You must "feed" it the information that you want it to extract the analysis from and then start prompting it for solutions. If you don't, your answers might not even be available because of the application's limitations.

Therefore, the first thing you must do is separate the information that you find that will be useful for your business. This can range from news stories, to studies, or even blog posts that you identify with the tone that is used. Since there is no "upload" feature in ChatGPT, you will need to copy and paste the text accordingly so that it can read the information. On the positive side, there is no specific "limit" to the number of information that you will use.

In addition to this, you might need to select the documents carefully and ensure that they have the specific keywords you are going to need. Once you have selected the needed information, copy and paste them by numbering the documents that will be used. Finally, once you are done, you can start "training" the brain so that the information it will give you is the one that you need. Here, I want to pause and remind you that any information that you add to ChatGPT may be stored in its database for future use and training and, therefore, you should be careful about adding sensitive and proprietary information that might be confidential and to which other parties should not have access to.

Training the Brain

Now that all the information has been fed to ChatGPT, it will be time to explain to it what you want it to do. You will need to prompt it by using the specific keywords as well as guideline, instructions, and parameters that it should use to fulfill your request. Even though you are able to ask generic questions, the more information you provide the more accurate the response will be.

Furthermore, if you provide sources that are written by you or some other party and correctly identify them, ChatGPT will be able to mimic the style and tone of writing to ensure that it meets your expectations. While this will work mostly for text-based content, if you have some coding knowledge, it is possible to "adjust" the application with speech-to-text information, for example, for more comprehensive teaching. Suppose you have recorded a lesson and you want a summary of what was said. This means that you could add the audio through code to ChatGPT and it would transcribe it and then give you the summary.

One of the most important things here is to experiment and be sure that you correctly tag the information so that ChatGPT can understand what you want. Once this has been done, you have effectively "trained" the application and will now be able to use it. You have reached the final part of the job, which is unleashing its potential to help you and your business.

Unleashing the Brain

After all the information has been inserted and you have trained the application, it is time to start prompting it to help you with your business. As you have seen in the previous chapter, the **manner** by which the questions are asked will have a huge difference in the output you will have. As you have seen in the previous chapter, the answer you will have will depend on how specific you are regarding the different questions. This means that if you have a special target group in mind for an ad, for example, it is essential that you feed ChatGPT this information so it can provide the best solution for you. To make sure that you are provided with the best possible information, read on to learn how to "speak" ChatGPT's language.

LEARNING TO SPEAK TO CHATGPT

When you think about asking ChatGPT for information, you should be sure that you provide as much context as possible for the answers to be accurate. Here, you should imagine that you are speaking to someone who has no knowledge at all about what you are talking about and, therefore, instead of typing in long sentences and using complicated words, try to keep it short and simple. You must ensure that there is a clear goal of what you want to extract from it to make it easier to identify any potential problems.

MrNewq (2023) suggests what they call "magic words" to make sure that the output to your prompt is as accurate as possible. This means adding to your question terms such as "let's think step-by-step" or "think aloud" and other phrases that can tell ChatGPT that what you really want is a detailed explanation that you can understand. This technique is referred to in the technology world as **prompt engineering**. When you carry out prompt engineering with an AI tool, you are training it and extracting from it the information according to your needs, which is why there is "prompt" in the word.

One of the things that you must always keep in mind is its NLP characteristics, which means that it will respond better if you are using natural language to prompt it. This does not mean you cannot be creative and original in your approach. However, it does mean that you should try to avoid as much as possible any typos in the text that you are prompting and that you try to be as direct as possible. Since ChatGPT does not have feelings (remember, it is a machine), it cannot determine the intention of what is being said with precision.

This means that while it can analyze the sentence structure and make deductions based on the choice of word pattern, it is unlikely that it will be able to understand implicit sarcasm in the prompt. You should then consider that in these cases using ChatGPT should be as straightforward as possible. On the other hand, remember that not all the information that ChatGPT contains in its database is bias-free. Therefore, some of the answers you may get for some prompts might not be as neutral as you would expect them to be. For this reason, even though you are going to use ChatGPT to help you with your business, you must always review the information that it gives you to ensure that there won't be a problem.

Finally, now that you know this, I want you to go back a few pages and look at the model questions that I have given you as examples in the previous chapters. If you tried them in ChatGPT, you must have noticed that their quality is alarmingly different and that the answers for the more specific questions are more accurate than the others you have asked. Although we are going to look more into detail how to do this in the next chapter (and I will even use some examples of what you can ask), my suggestion is that you take some time to reflect on what you will prompt. You should prepare the information on demographics, for example, so you can give it accurate parameters on the required target group.

WHAT YOU CAN DO WITH THIS METHOD

If you are an active LinkedIn user and are tuned with the latest updates in the market regarding the AI business, you might have heard about a company created by Portuguese entrepreneur João Ferrão dos Santos using ChatGPT4. The company, named AIstethic Apparel, was created by prompting the AI application and asking it to make the business decisions—from the company name and product to the information that would be released to the public. This journey was registered on the social media platform as Mr. dos Santos prompted the tool and proved that you can build a business by using ChatGPT.

Now, what I want to say with this is not that you should follow the same steps and depend exclusively on AI to work on your business for you. I want to show you that it is possible to use the application in a way that will be beneficial when you add your "human" input to it. From calculating financial ratios, analyzing financial statements, and forecasting financial trends to aiding you with hiring and recruitment advice, you can rely on ChatGPT to be your official assistant as you build or revamp your business.

Looking at the Different Departments of a Business

1. **Human resources:** One of the first departments you can use ChatGPT with is human resources. While it will not help you with payroll and some specific administrative tasks, it will help you to write job descriptions. By correctly prompting the application, you will be able to create a description with the skills you need, the experience level required, and any specific information that your business requests. Even if you have prompted and trained it before, you will be able to ask it "Can you develop a position for HR training analyst based on the characteristics of my company?" for example. In addition to this, you will also be able to create job descriptions that mimic the

tone you are using for your business'
communication and even develop others that
are gender-neutral, making them more
appealing to the market and directed at the
group that you are targeting for this specific
position.

2. **IT:** If you do not have an IT department, you
can use ChatGPT as an initial alternative to
troubleshoot technology problems that you
might be having and save a few dollars in the
process. Furthermore, if you have a website that
is in English and you are expanding the
business to a different country, you can use
ChatGPT's translation tool to help you
translate the content for your website, for
example. This will also help you to save some
money because all you will need is for someone
to review the work that the application did,
instead of having someone translate it from
scratch, which can be more expensive.

3. **Marketing and internal communication:** This
is one of the areas in which you will see
ChatGPT shine and make a difference. By using
the application, you can create SEO articles that
will take a larger audience to your content in
search engines and quickly create email
campaigns for your customers. One of the

many advantages of using ChatGPT for communication is that it will give you content that, although might not have a "personal" touch to it, will be free of errors and structurally correct. After this is done, all you will need to do is review the content and make any adjustments that you see necessary. In addition to this, you can have the communication be written mimicking a specific tone, such as a memo from the CEO or from HR, for example, which can be different in structure but with the same intent.

4. **Customer experience:** If you are having trouble targeting a specific audience, you can ask ChatGPT to help you with the tone of the message you want to send. In addition to this, several companies have started incorporating the application into their website chatbots to increase customer experience. Most of the time, customers are not happy to talk to a machine that has automated answers and can become frustrated at standardized responses that do not meet their needs. By adding a service like ChatGPT to "speak" to your clients once it has been dutifully trained, you will see that customers will feel more comfortable to speak to a machine that has human-like answers.

5. **Financial analysis:** Although no machine can fully replace human advice, especially when it concerns your money, ChatGPT is fully able to help you in calculating financial ratios, analyzing financial statements, and forecasting financial trends. Furthermore, while it is unable to create the drawing of a table for you, it is possible to input the data that you would like it to analyze and have it draw a text-based table that you can copy and paste in the program of your preference. This will be a helpful tool for those moments in which you want to determine estimates or even create potential profitable products, as you will now see.

6. **Product creation and innovation:** Brainstorming is one of the features that ChatGPT has that will make your life so much easier. Suppose that you work with only one product and you want to expand your portfolio. You can feed the application with the information on your business as well as those pertaining to market trends and use it to help you think what your best options are. In addition to this, if you need to create a business plan, ChatGPT can help you do this by giving you all the steps and information that you will need to analyze and determine the next steps of

your project. This will be a great help for innovating your services or products and will help you keep up-to-date with the market you work with.

7. **Administrative tasks:** No more need to waste your time thinking about how to set up a presentation for potential investors and clients. By using ChatGPT, you can ask it to create the text for the presentation you need to give based on the audience and all you will need to do is to copy, paste, and format the content. In addition to this, you can carry out several other tasks such as answering emails, summarizing long texts, and preparing an agenda for your day.

All these features and tools that you have seen in this section are native to ChatGPT. As you can see, just these are already of great help for you and your business if you feed it the adequate information and give it specific instructions on what you want.

However, once ChatGPT was released in the market, developers and other companies were fast to develop what are known as "extensions" so that the AI tool could work with items that are **not** native to it. When I say that these extensions are not native, I refer to programs that were not developed by OpenAI and that are a part of ChatGPTs variety of tools.

As you will see in the last section of this chapter before we start practicing, there are several of these extensions that are available according to the navigator you use and that will give you an even bigger advantage. The best part? Most of them are free to install and will only need your authorization to do so. If you are ready to be even more in awe of the things that are possible with ChatGPT, keep reading and you will see there is more —much, much more!

BONUS: NON-NATIVE FEATURES AND EXTENSIONS

Sometimes, all we want is to have a little extra time on our hands and even though this can be done by effortlessly using ChatGPT, the process of copying and pasting information can be quite confusing. This is why **extensions** exist and are an excellent tool to download and have in your computer. Apart from being mostly free, when you install these extensions in your browser you will see that it will automatically connect to ChatGPT and make your life easier by not having to copy and paste the information from one window to the other.

One of these tools promises to make the problem of only having updated information up to 2021 easier. When you install ChatGPT for Google, for example, the extension will enable you to have answers to all the searches that you make without needing to change tabs. In addition to this, the extension is not only used for Google but for several other browsers with the same quality. Essentially speaking, what you will do is type in a query in the browser and the answer will be given to you by ChatGPT in the same screen where the research was carried out.

Another extension that can do a similar action is WebChatGPT. This tool, when turned on, will enable ChatGPT to search the internet for the information you are requiring and overcome its database limitations. However, different from ChatGPT for Google, the action will be carried out in the ChatGPT window, where you will be able to prompt it for more information as you go. The information searched will be compiled and summarized based on the most relevant results and can be turned on and off as you wish for more or less input from the AI tool.

A different extension promises to use ChatGPT to summarize YouTube videos that you want to learn more from. With YouTube Summary, you will be able to ask for the transcript of the video you are watching and it will be automatically redirected to ChatGPT. Once the video has finished, you will be able to prompt ChatGPT to do a summary of the content and give you the main highlights. This will also ensure that you have accurate information and is a different way of "feeding" information into the AI tool and giving more content for the Business Brain Method.

Now, if your issue is with writing posts directly into social media channels or replying to emails, there are several extensions available in the market that will enable you to do this. Some of these tools include ChatGPT Writer, that will help you write emails and messages based on the selected content without needing to copy and paste the information, TweetGPT, that does the same for Twitter, and ChatSonic, that can be used across different internet features, including interacting with LinkedIn, Instagram, and Facebook.

Finally, if your issue is typing and you would prefer to use voice to communicate with ChatGPT, you can download either the Prometheus or the Talk-to-ChatGPT, both which will allow you to use voice commands to speak to the AI tool. Once you install them, be sure that your computer microphone is on so that you can prompt by using voice and you will see the answer appear in the ChatGPT screen. The main difference between both tools is that the first will give you the answer back in text, while Talk-to-ChatGPT will also give you the option of listening to the answer ChatGPT will give you.

Now you are **really** fully equipped to use ChatGPT, right? In addition to its native features, if you want to explore the possibilities that go beyond it, it is also possible. However, since not all of these are free for the user or some people might not feel comfortable using them, I will prepare you and show you an example on how to use ChatGPT Business Brain Method in the next chapter only by using its **native** features. As you read, I suggest that you keep your computer open next to you so that you can also try out the exercises and see what kinds of answers you will get.

Are you ready to get to work? Read on and let's get started!

FROM CHATGPT TO BUSINESS BRAIN

W hen you think about the impact that ChatGPT is having in worldwide business, you might understand the reason why Microsoft wants to increase its partnership with the company and invest $10 billion in the next few years (Tellez, 2023). Some of these companies include the consumer giant Shopify, the language app Duolingo, SnapChat application and the financial giant Morgan Stanley. While these companies have seen advantages in integrating the AI tool to its operations, others do not seem so excited to do so.

Apart from the education institutions that I have already mentioned that are not at all happy with this development, several banks such as Bank of America and Deutsche Bank have restricted the use of the tool by their employees because of safety reasons. Also on the other part of the market is Amazon, who has also established limits on how ChatGPT can be used and to which situation they can be applied. And these are only to mention a few of the companies that are contrary to its application in the business world.

However, for the companies that **are** using ChatGPT, they are incorporating the application in the most varied ways that include improvement of the software coding to managing external communications. As I mentioned in the previous chapter, all of these uses are possible if you are willing to take your time and learn about the tool. Now, without further delay, let's get into a practical example of how you can use the Brain Business Method with ChatGPT.

HOW TO USE THE BUSINESS BRAIN METHOD WITH CHATGPT

As you have seen in the previous chapter, training ChatGPT on the information pertaining to your business will be essential for you to succeed in using it for business advice. In this phase of the Business Brain Method, you will be teaching the application by using the same method applied by its developers. When you select the data that you are going to use to train ChatGPT, you must take a few items into consideration such as:

- **Set clear objectives:** The first and most important thing that you need to do before implementing the Business Brain Method is to know what you are going to do. You must have an objective or an idea of what you want and what are your expectations. You can do this by brainstorming using the traditional pen and paper and then prompt ChatGPT to help you refine the ideas or you can use ChatGPT to help you brainstorm. In this aspect, having a tool that will use NLP will be an incredible advantage because you will also be able to prompt it to ask you questions and define what your final goal is. The main thing here is that you only start prompting ChatGPT once you have the bigger picture of what you want for your business so that it does not get confused with too many ideas and ends up giving you vague information that you might not use.

- **Tell ChatGPT what you are going to do:** One good practice to put in place is to inform ChatGPT of what you are going to do. For example, if you are going to feed it information on an existing business, it might be interesting to prompt it by saying that you are looking for help in your business and that you are going to upload information so that it can help you think about strategies. This will enable the tool to wait and not immediately respond. You can also add sentences such as "I am going to give you information. Please wait until I ask you a question to respond" so that it is not immediately bringing you outputs to what you enter.

- **Pick the correct information:** When you are searching for the information to feed ChatGPT, be sure that you are using reliable sources and data. This will be essential to guarantee that you will not be given any incorrect data or that your output is not precise. One of the basic ways to do this, if you already have a website, for example, is to convert all the information in the website into text and copy and paste it in the chat window. Be sure to remove links and text that will be irrelevant, such as the name of the company that created the website, for example, and any links to other pages. If you don't have a website yet, you could insert the information contained in your business plan so that it has an idea of what you want to do.

- **The more information, the better:** Just as anything you want to learn more about in life, the more information you feed to ChatGPT, the more it will have to base its analysis on.

Therefore, if you are talking about a product, you might want to add your thoughts and ideas, as well as data on how your business has been performing so the analysis can be more complete. This step is crucial that will enable you to "train the brain" with the additional information that you will need. Remember that one of the best features of ChatGPT is its brainstorming ideas, so take advantage of this capability and provide it with statistics, data, and as many unbiased facts as possible to ensure a positive and comprehensive result.

- **Identify your writing style:** Many people want their businesses to "be their face." Due to this, it is important that you provide ChatGPT with as many samples as possible so that it can identify what it is you want your text to look like. When you do this, remember to identify the text with phrases such as "this is a sample of the writing style I want" or "this is my writing style, can you identify what it is?" When you do this, you will be able to understand and determine if the text that ChatGPT will generate meets the standard that you are looking for or if some changes will be needed. Some examples of this could be "add more humor," "add more sarcasm," or "speak in simpler terms."

- **Identify your target audience:** For a business to be successful, it is essential that you are able to identify the target audience that you want to reach. This can be done in two ways: the first is that you already have this specific group in mind and you will request ChatGPT to adjust its responses based on them (internal or external). The second is that you are still developing and thinking about the business that you are going to build and you prompt ChatGPT to help you identify what is the best target audience for your product. After this is done, you can even prompt it to adjust the language it is using so that members of this group can better identify with your brand. One suggestion that I make here is that, if you have a target group in mind, search for content that these individuals are attracted to on the internet and feed it to the application so it has updated information.

- **Make a list of questions:** Once you have everything ready and a clear idea of what you want, you will start feeding the brain with more information. To make this an easier process for you, write down a list of questions of the subjects you need assistance with and the things that you want more information on. Having a clear list of questions that will be asked will also help you to be more specific on what you are asking from it, giving you better and more detailed answers. You do not need to input these questions in the first moment, we will do this in the last part of the process, when you are "unleashing the brain," when you will effectively prompt it for content.

Now that you have the basic information out of the way, I will give you a step-by-step template of how you will input the information and how the Business Brain Method will work. My suggestion here, although I will be giving you some of the input to the application, is that you keep a notebook or your computer nearby so you can start writing down some ideas that we will later use to practice.

Feeding the Brain

As you know, the first step of the Business Brain Method is to feed ChatGPT with relevant information. This will include searching the internet for the relevant information and separating it into topics relating to each of the areas that you will use them for. This first part of the process is divided into two parts:

- Decide what content you want to produce and the application that you will use it for.
- Find specific samples you want ChatGPT to replicate and copy the exact text and paste it in the ChatGPT window.

  ○ Clean up the text and remove any unnecessary and irrelevant bits of text.
  ○ If you want it to produce an output similar to your writing style, provide it with a few examples so it can analyze the information. If you want it to respond like an expert, prompt it telling it to "think like an expert." If you have children as a target audience, use the phrase "pretend you are speaking to a child and explain this topic" and so on.

Now that you have fed it the information it will need, more specifically that pertaining to your business or your idea, it is time to train the brain to "think" like you and the target customers the products will be presented to.

Training the Brain

When you are training the brain, the first thing you will do is to use a prompt to ask it for something. Now, you remember when I said that you need to tell ChatGPT what you want it to do or the "role" that you want it to mimic? Well, this is where this part comes in and will be essential to the process. This second stage of the Business Brain Method is also composed of two parts and, to make it easier to understand, I will give you an example of a prompt you can use, for which you will just need to fill in the information between brackets ([]).

- Use the prompt:

  Today, you are going to be a world-class direct response copywriter who specializes in writing [content type]. I'm going to show you [X] examples of good [content type]. Just read them. Don't explain them to me. After you acknowledge that you've read all [X] examples, I will give you further instructions. Ready?

- Once ChatGPT replies, feed it the text with the information you want it to mimic or use as an example.

  - If you are feeding it multiple examples, specify which numbered example you're feeding it.
  - If you want it to wait until you have finished adding all the information, be sure to ask it to do so. Tell it you need it to respond only after you are done inputting the information.

○ You can also add comments regarding each of the samples that you are feeding to tell the application exactly what it is that you want.

By giving it examples of what you want it to do, you will essentially be training ChatGPT to think like you want it to. However, one of the things you must remember is to change the "voice" that is used for each of the instances so it matches the situation. If you don't do this, it is possible that it will continue to mimic the same tone and you might mix up the "message written by the CEO" and the "message written by the marketing team."

As you can see in step 3, you are telling it once again what to do and what you expect from it. The same will happen to the tone of the output. Since ChatGPT can use several tones to write the same message, use this to your advantage and prompt it to do small and specific modifications that might suit you and your business better. Once you have reached what you consider the ideal tone, let ChatGPT know that this is what you want for the future outputs. If you are talking about more than one, remember to "give them names" or label them, so that it can understand the different voices you are using.

Unleashing the Brain

The final step of the process, when you will "unleash the brain" has finally arrived and, once more, it consists of two steps.

- Instruct ChatGPT to write your content using this prompt:

Remember, you're acting as a world-class direct response copywriter who specializes in [content type]. Now write me [X] more [content type] that follows a similar structure. Make them sensational and emotionally engaging.

- Edit and optimize.

You have successfully completed your first prompt to ChatGPT and generated your first content! Congratulations! How does that feel? I bet you are already excited about the possibilities that you have identified and the different approaches that you can take into making your business thrive.

Checking the Work

Now that you have completed the first trial, I want to make a few important observations regarding the last step of the process, editing and optimizing. As everything, you must be careful not to simply copy and paste the output that ChatGPT gives you into the communication channel that you are using. It is important that you review the information, especially because ChatGPT is known for not being the most concise and direct writing tool. Here are a few things to remember when you are proofreading or correcting the content generated by the application.

- **Factual accuracy:** This may sound weird to you but you should know that, sometimes, ChatGPT lies. Yes, you read this correctly. And eventually, it might get some wrong information. Yes, this is a true possibility. This means that you have to be extra careful about the content that you are using based on its output. Remember to always check your facts and review the information that it is giving you to make sure that it is accurate. Carry out a quick internet search to ensure that everything is correct, especially if you are basing the content of the message based on facts. Can't hurt to be sure!
- **Grammar and spelling:** ChatGPT's primary language is English and this is the language that it was trained on. While this means that most of its grammar and spelling might be correct, be

sure to carry out a small check, especially if you are using foreign or technical jargon. In addition to this, if you are going to use ChatGPT in another language, remember that it is available because it presents good results, but not an accuracy as well as the one presented in English. Therefore, if you will use it for translation or to write in another language, be sure to check the overall content of the message with someone who can identify if there are any mistakes.

- **Overall style:** Even though ChatGPT can be very efficient in mimicking the style that you desire for the text you request, it is always good to check the overall style and ensure that it is according to what you expect. Sometimes, because we are talking about a machine, it might lack some personalization, such as speaking directly to the audience or adding a bit of emotion to the text. If you are talking about a message that has a specific intention, such as marketing campaigns, it might be useful to double check the style with some other people to ensure that it is not offensive or biased against certain groups.

- **Readability:** As I mentioned earlier, ChatGPT can be quite wordy. When you think about this in readability terms, it can mean that the audience might find it difficult to understand the point you are trying to make or get bored with the content. Be sure to eliminate redundancies that might negatively impact the audience and make the answer as concise as possible. Adapt the message to be direct and effective, instead of long and complicated. One of the remarks I should make here is that when you ask ChatGPT for specific information, you can also ask it to write it down using bullet points or numbers, making it easier to understand. Finally, it will generally give an overview or "conclusion" of the content that is mostly repetitive, so you might want to consider cutting that part off if this is what it suggests.

- **Matching tone and voice:** If you are prompting ChatGPT to write a message to the shareholders of your company, the tone and voice that will be used is completely different than the one you would use in a marketing campaign. Can you think about what the impact would be if you mistakenly mixed up the two and sent each of them the message intended to the other group? This could potentially cause an embarrassing situation.

Therefore, always be sure to tone-check the information and ensure that the message is appropriate in tone and voice to the audience to which it is intended.

PRACTICE

Now, it's your turn! I have given you all the tips and steps to effectively use the Business Brain Method and I think it is time for you to give it a try. To do this, I want you to open up ChatGPT on your computer if you still haven't done so. Think about your own business or a made-up scenario that you would like to test. Since this is practice, you might want to use a simple situation that will not require too much research to identify the data that you will feed the application.

Use the information you have been given in the past two chapters to execute the three stages of the Business Brain Method and see how you do. Simulate preparing an SEO ad, a marketing campaign, and even developing a new brand. Talk about the expected financials and ask about the good and bad points of the market. The sky is your limit. If you are talking about more current issues, remember to use updated information or ChatGPT might not recognize it. Maybe you could even try setting up an email message mimicking the tone of a famous person. It is all up to you!

The point of this exercise is not to effectively start working on your business now (we still have some ground to cover here!), but to get you used to the method. By doing this, you will start getting more comfortable and be able to identify the points that you need more practice and how your prompting is working. Take some time! Test the Business Brain Method. Be creative! Once you are done, come back because we will now start talking about how ChatGPT can be useful in other areas of your life. Happy testing and see you in a bit!

Help Others Boost Their Profits Easily, Affordably, and Immediately With ChatGPT

"Technology is best when it brings people together."

— *MATT MULLENWEG*

Earlier in the book, I mentioned that ChatGPT is the buzzword in a myriad of sectors, ranging from manufacturing to sales, customer service, and marketing.

Thus far, you have seen the myriad of ways in which ChatGPT can facilitate a wide range of tasks, with some of its most impressive abilities including automated text generation, text summaries, answering questions, and even explaining and writing code.

I also shared the fact that while some users are embracing ChatGPT and finding new ways that this tool can enhance everything from customer service to marketing resources, others are more reluctant to try it out.

Some fear that ChatGPT is complicated to use, or that you need to spend money to harness its benefits. However, benefiting from ChatGPT is as easy as asking it your first pertinent question, and it won't cost you a dime to do so.

I wrote this book so business owners can feel more confident about ChatGPT and understand the full extent to which it can boost their productivity and make processes more efficient.

In Chapter Four, we discussed the key strategies involved in feeding, training, and unleashing the "business brain." We also mentioned that one of the most important skills to hone when using ChatGPT is knowing the right prompts to use so that it provides you with detailed, purposeful answers. By caring out prompt engineering, you train and extract information according to your needs, dramatically cutting the time and effort you need to perform various tasks.

So many businesses are raving about what ChatGPT can do for them. Companies like Salesforce, Microsoft, Slack, and many more have openly shared the myriad of ways in which they are using ChatGPT.

Even if you have a small business or you are a budding startup, you can share the useful things you have discovered about ChatGPT. You can help others overcome their fear of the unknown and show how easily ChatGPT can maximize the efforts of their teams.

By leaving a review of this book on Amazon, you can share the guidance that other business owners need

to train ChatGPT to provide the specific answers they are seeking.

When you leave your honest opinion of this book and how it's helped you on Amazon, other readers will be inspired to employ ChatGPT in a host of functions, ranging from Human Resources to content generation for their blog.

Thank you for helping business people like you find the information they're looking for. Together, we can ensure that companies embrace the technologies that can make them more profitable and efficient.

Scan the QR code to leave a review!

PART III

USING CHATGPT TO SUPERCHARGE YOUR LIFE

BOOSTING BUSINESS PRODUCTIVITY AND EFFICIENCY

A s you have seen so far, ChatGPT provides its users with several benefits that make it an attractive tool to use in the workplace. Recent surveys indicate that almost 50% of employees use ChatGPT to aid them with their daily activities such as writing emails, coding, and copywriting—and this includes those that are working for big companies such as Nike, Twitter, Google, and IBM, among others (Gupta, 2023a). Nevertheless, some people are still reluctant to admit using it for their daily work activities. According to Jackson (2023), 68% of the people who claimed to use the application to help them with work do it without their superiors knowing about it.

If almost half of the market is doing this, there is no problem in me doing it as well, right? But since you are beginning your journey with this tool, in this chapter I am going to show you some practical uses of ChatGPT and even give you a few of the prompts you can use to obtain the needed information. For this to happen, so that we have a guide to follow, I am going to create an imaginary business and show you how the prompts should be used to their best advantage. Are you ready?

OUR IMAGINARY BUSINESS

For our imaginary business, we are going to use the example of developing a bakery. In our bakery, we will have sweet and salty products as well as normal and gluten-free items. We are just beginning the process of building the brand and we still don't have marketing material, personnel—nothing. The name of our business will be *1, 2, 3 Bakeree*. We are going to use ChatGPT to help us build the business and prepare everything you will need to start off. The first stop is creating marketing and sales documents to make sure that you reach the largest number of customers possible.

As you already know, the first thing is that you will need to tell ChatGPT what you want to do and how you expect it to help you. My suggested prompt is:

- I am building a business and would like your help to set it up. It will be a bakery that sells sweet and salty products and that has normal and gluten-free products. The name of the business is 1, 2, 3 Bakeree. We are going to start with developing a marketing and sales strategy.

ChatGPT output:

Great! Developing a solid marketing and sales strategy is crucial for the success of any business, especially when starting out. Here are some steps to consider:

1. Define your target market: Before you start marketing your bakery, it's essential to define your target market. Who are your ideal customers? Are they health-conscious individuals, people with dietary restrictions, families, or young adults? Once you have a clear understanding of your target market, you can tailor your marketing efforts to their needs and preferences.

2. Conduct market research: Conducting market research will help you understand your target market's preferences and behavior, as well as your competitors' strengths and weaknesses. You can conduct surveys, focus groups, or online research to gather information.

3. Develop a brand identity: A strong brand identity can help differentiate your bakery from competitors and create a strong connection with your target market. Your brand identity should include your logo, color scheme, messaging, and overall aesthetic.

4. Develop a marketing plan: Based on your market research and brand identity, develop a marketing plan that outlines your marketing goals, strategies, and tactics. Your marketing plan should include both online and offline marketing efforts such as social media marketing, email marketing, content marketing, influencer marketing, events, and promotions.

5. Set sales goals: Setting sales goals can help you track your progress and measure the success of your marketing efforts. Your sales goals should be specific, measurable, attainable, relevant, and time-bound.

6. Develop a sales strategy: Your sales strategy should outline how you plan to sell your products and services to your target market. This may include setting up a website, using e-commerce platforms, attending events and farmer's markets, collaborating with other businesses, or offering special promotions.

7. Implement and track: Once you have developed your marketing and sales strategy, it's time to implement it and track your results. Monitor your sales data, track your marketing efforts, and adjust your strategy as needed.

Remember that marketing and sales are ongoing efforts, and it may take some time to see results. Consistency and persistence are key to building a successful business. Good luck with your bakery, and feel free to reach out if you have any further questions!

- Next, we are going to inform them that we are going to ask them some questions with the prompt: I am going to ask you some questions to build the sales and marketing plan so you can help with the process.

ChatGPT output:

Sure, I'll be happy to help you answer any questions you have to develop your sales and marketing plan. Please go ahead and ask your questions!

MARKETING AND SALES

Since marketing and sales is what is going to drive your company, or in this case, the 1, 2, 3 Bakeree, we are going to start by prompting Chat GPT to help us with the marketing plan for the business. In addition to this, we are going to see the different ways that it responds to the prompts according to the format that we request it to write. Just as you have seen before, each of the bullet points will be a different prompt for a marketing feature and I will place the ChatGPT output right after it.

Planning and Writing Copy in Different Formats

- **SEO content:** Write me a short 300-SEO article that will help the users find the bakery in their web searches. You should include the main products that the brand features and it should target a younger public.

ChatGPT output:

Looking for a bakery that offers delicious sweet and salty treats for a young and trendy crowd? Look no further than 1, 2, 3 Bakeree!

At 1, 2, 3 Bakeree, we specialize in creating baked goods that are perfect for young people who love to indulge in treats that are both delicious and Instagram-worthy. Our bakery offers a wide variety of sweet and salty products that will satisfy any craving.

If you have a sweet tooth, you'll love our selection of cupcakes, cakes, and pastries. Our skilled bakers use only the finest ingredients to create treats that are not only tasty but also beautiful to look at. Whether you're looking for a classic chocolate cake or a unique flavor like matcha or lavender, we've got you covered.

For those who prefer savory snacks, we also offer a selection of savory pastries and sandwiches. Our croissants and quiches are perfect for a quick breakfast or lunch, while our paninis and baguettes are the perfect choice for a filling and delicious sandwich.

At 1, 2, 3 Bakeree, we believe that everyone should be able to enjoy our delicious treats, which is why we offer both normal and gluten-free options. Whether you have dietary restrictions or simply prefer gluten-free products, you'll find a wide variety of options at our bakery.

So what are you waiting for? Come visit us today and indulge in the sweet and savory treats that 1, 2, 3 Bakeree has to offer. Our bakery is the perfect choice for young people who love to treat themselves to delicious and trendy baked goods.

- **SEO Keyword Search:** What are some essential keywords I should use to attract the public and see what my competitors are doing?

ChatGPT output:

Here are some essential keywords you can use to attract potential customers and see what your competitors are doing:

1. Bakery
2. Sweet treats
3. Savory snacks
4. Gluten-free
5. Desserts
6. Cakes
7. Pastries
8. Bread
9. Coffee
10. Tea
11. Breakfast
12. Lunch
13. Snacks
14. Local bakery
15. Gourmet bakery
16. Artisan bakery
17. Organic bakery
18. Freshly baked
19. Family-owned bakery
20. Specialty bakery

To see what your competitors are doing, you can search for these keywords on search engines like Google or Bing, and look at the websites and social media pages of other bakeries in your area. You can also use tools like SEMrush or Ahrefs to analyze your competitors' websites and see which keywords they are targeting.

- **Video scripts:** Now, I want to create a 15-second video for a commercial on television and the internet. The ad will air in the morning on television and will be used in my webpage as a part of the marketing strategy. Write me a script that will help make the video

ChatGPT output:

[The video opens with a shot of a beautiful display of 1, 2, 3 Bakeree's sweet and savory products.]

Narrator (voiceover): "Are you looking for a bakery that offers delicious treats that are perfect for any occasion?"

[The video shows a young person taking a bite of a cupcake or pastry.]

Narrator (voiceover): "1, 2, 3 Bakeree has got you covered. Our baked goods are not only delicious but also beautiful to look at."

[The video shows a person taking a bite of a savory pastry or sandwich.]

Narrator (voiceover): "Whether you're in the mood for something sweet or savory, we've got the perfect treat for you."

[The video shows a person holding a gluten-free product.]

Narrator (voiceover): "Plus, we also offer a wide variety of gluten-free options for those with dietary restrictions."

[The video ends with a shot of the bakery's logo and a call to action.]

Narrator (voiceover): "Come visit us today and discover the delicious treats that 1, 2, 3 Bakeree has to offer."

This script can be adapted to showcase specific products and highlight any current promotions or deals that 1, 2, 3 Bakeree may be offering. The key is to keep the message short and engaging, and to emphasize the quality and variety of the bakery's products.

- **Email marketing:** I have a list of 200 friends, family and neighbors who live near the bakery. I want to attract them to the opening of the bakery but, more specifically, I want them to attract them to come in the afternoon after lunch, when it is our least busy hour. Write me an email marketing message with 100 words that is short and sweet.

ChatGPT output:

Dear [Recipient],

We're excited to announce the opening of 1, 2, 3 Bakeree, and we'd love for you to join us for a sweet treat or savory snack! As a valued member of our community, we'd like to invite you to visit us during our least busy hour, in the afternoon after lunch.

Come and indulge in our delicious cupcakes, cakes, and pastries, or enjoy a savory croissant or sandwich. Plus, we also offer a variety of gluten-free options for those with dietary restrictions.

Our bakery is conveniently located in your neighborhood, and we'd love to see you there! Bring your friends and family along, and make it a fun afternoon treat. We promise you won't be disappointed.

Thank you for your support, and we look forward to seeing you soon!

Best regards,

[Your Name]

- **Additional prompt:** I like it, but I don't want the customers to know that this is the least busy hour. I want to attract them for afternoon coffee with friends or for a break in the afternoon.

ChatGPT Output:

Dear [Recipient],

We're thrilled to announce the opening of 1, 2, 3 Bakeree, and we'd love for you to join us for a sweet or savory treat during your afternoon break. Our bakery is conveniently located in your neighborhood, and we offer a wide variety of delicious cupcakes, cakes, pastries, croissants, sandwiches, and more.

Whether you're looking for a quiet spot to catch up with friends over a cup of coffee or tea, or simply need a sweet pick-me-up in the middle of the day, we've got you covered. Plus, we also offer a variety of gluten-free options for those with dietary restrictions.

Our bakery is the perfect spot to relax, unwind, and enjoy some delicious treats. We promise you won't be disappointed!

Thank you for your support, and we look forward to welcoming you to 1, 2, 3 Bakeree soon!

Best regards,

[Your Name]

Remember to include all relevant information, such as the bakery's address, opening hours, and any promotions or discounts that you may be offering. You may also want to include a call to action, such as asking recipients to bring a friend along or to share the message with their friends and family.

- **Product descriptions:** There are several products in the bakery and I am creating a menu with each of their descriptions. Can you create the product descriptions for these products including that they all come in the normal and in the gluten-free format? The products are: Chocolate croissant, carrot cake, red velvet muffins, and cheese and ham rolls.

ChatGPT output:

Chocolate Croissant:

1. Our flaky, buttery croissant filled with rich and delicious chocolate is the perfect indulgence for any time of day. Whether you enjoy it as a breakfast pastry, afternoon snack or dessert, our chocolate croissant is sure

to satisfy your cravings. We also offer a gluten-free option for those with dietary restrictions.

Carrot Cake:

2. Our moist and delicious carrot cake is made with fresh carrots, spices, and a decadent cream cheese frosting. With just the right amount of sweetness and a touch of crunch from the nuts, our carrot cake is a crowd-pleaser. We also offer a gluten-free version of this classic cake, so everyone can enjoy it.

Red Velvet Muffins:

3. Our red velvet muffins are moist, fluffy, and have just the right amount of cocoa flavor. Topped with a sweet cream cheese frosting and a sprinkle of red velvet crumbs, these muffins are a delicious treat. Plus, we offer a gluten-free option, so you can enjoy them without worrying about dietary restrictions.

Cheese and Ham Rolls:

4. Our cheese and ham rolls are the perfect savory snack or light lunch option. Our fluffy and soft bread is filled with a savory mixture of cheese and ham, making it the perfect combination of flavors. We also offer a gluten-free option, so you can enjoy them no matter your dietary needs.

We hope these descriptions help to entice your customers and showcase the delicious and diverse offerings available at 1, 2, 3 Bakeree!

- **Sales pages:** I am also creating a website that I want to be user friendly and with easy to read information. In the page, I want the user to be able to see our prices, pictures of the products and an easy way to access the store. How do you suggest I create the sales page?

ChatGPT output:

Great! Here are some suggestions for creating a user-friendly sales page for your bakery:

1. Use a clean and simple design: Keep the design of your website clean and simple, with plenty of white space and a consistent color scheme. Use high-quality images of your products to showcase their deliciousness.
2. Display prices clearly: Make sure your prices are easy to find and read on your sales page. Consider grouping similar products together and displaying the prices in a clear and organized manner.
3. Include product descriptions: Provide a short and sweet description of each product that

highlights its key features, such as its flavor, texture, and any dietary restrictions. Make sure the descriptions are easy to read and understand.

4. Offer an easy way to order: Make it easy for your customers to place an order online by including a clear and prominent "Order Now" button or link. You may also want to include your phone number or email address for those who prefer to place orders by phone or email.

5. Make it mobile-friendly: Ensure your website is mobile-friendly, meaning it's easy to navigate and read on a mobile device. This is especially important since many customers will likely be browsing your website on their phones or tablets.

6. Include customer reviews: Consider including customer reviews or testimonials on your sales page. This can help build trust and credibility with potential customers.

By following these tips, you can create a sales page that is user-friendly, easy to navigate, and highlights the best of what your bakery has to offer.

CUSTOMER SERVICE

As a business, it is essential that you are aware of the customer behavior and that you are ready to answer any suggestions and complaints that they make. Guess what? ChatGPT can help you with this too. It will help you answer client questions, reviews, and complaints, help you brainstorm ideas, and even send out information about changes in the products and services that you have. Here are some possible simulated situations for our fictional business.

Replying to Customer Complaints

- Prompt: I just had a client come to the bakery and complain that the images that they see on the website do not match the products you received in our bakery. How should I politely respond to them?

ChatGPT output:

I'm sorry to hear that your client had a negative experience. Here's an example of a polite response you could use:

Dear [Client Name],

Thank you for bringing this to our attention. We are sorry to hear that the images on our website did not match the products you received in our bakery. We take these concerns seriously and we want to make things right.

We strive to provide the highest quality products and we want every customer to have a positive experience. We apologize for any confusion or disappointment this may have caused you.

If you would like to discuss this matter further, please do not hesitate to contact us. We value your feedback and we appreciate your business.

Thank you,

[Your Name]

Remember to always stay polite, apologize for any inconvenience, and offer to discuss the matter further. This shows that you care about your customers' concerns and are willing to work to resolve any issues they may have.

- Prompt 2: I like the answer, but I need them to be aware that the pictures are different because there is a whole production behind them, including adding filters and other techniques. Can you add this to the response?

ChatGPT output:

Certainly! Here's a revised response that addresses your concern:

Dear [Client Name],

Thank you for bringing this to our attention. We are sorry to hear that the images on our website did not match the products you received in our bakery. We understand your frustration and we want to explain that there is a production process involved in creating the images on our website, including the use of filters and other techniques. However, we acknowledge that we should make every effort to ensure that the images accurately reflect our products.

We strive to provide the highest quality products and we want every customer to have a positive experience. We apologize for any confusion or disappointment this may have caused you.

If you would like to discuss this matter further or have any other concerns, please do not hesitate to contact us. We value your feedback and we appreciate your business.

Thank you,

[Your Name]

By explaining the process behind creating the images on your website, you are helping the customer understand why there may be differences between the images and the actual products. This helps to build trust and credibility with the customer.

Troubleshooting Ideas

- Prompt: I want to add a vegan line to our products, is this a good idea? Sales have been good for the regular and gluten-free products, but I am unsure if there will be a young vegan public to consume the products.

ChatGPT output:

Adding a vegan line to your products can be a great idea, especially as more and more people are choosing veganism for various reasons. While sales for your regular and gluten-free products have been good, introducing a vegan line could attract a new and growing demographic of health-conscious and eco-friendly consumers.

Additionally, having a vegan line can also increase the variety of options for your existing customers, some of whom may also be interested in trying vegan products. It can also set your bakery apart from competitors who do not offer vegan options.

Before introducing the vegan line, you can do some market research to identify the demand for such products in your area. You can also start with a smaller range of products and see how they are received by customers.

Overall, it can be a good idea to add a vegan line to your products, as long as it aligns with your business goals and values, and you do your due diligence in researching and testing the market.

Sending Out Notifications of Service Changes

- Prompt: I have decided to add the vegan product line together with the other products. But now I need to inform the customers of this change and possibility. I want you to create an attractive notification that our services have changed and that there is now this offering.

ChatGPT output:

"Dear valued customers,

We're excited to announce that we're expanding our product offerings to include a new vegan line! We understand the importance of providing options that cater to different dietary needs and lifestyles, and we're thrilled to introduce this new line to our bakery.

Our vegan line features the same high-quality ingredients and delicious flavors you've come to love from us, now with plant-based options that are perfect for those who follow a vegan diet or simply want to try something new.

We invite you to come and try our new vegan line, along with our other products that cater to your dietary needs, including normal and gluten-free options.

Thank you for your continued support and we hope to see you soon at 1, 2, 3 Bakeree!

Best regards,

[Your Name/Your Bakery]"

- Prompt 2: I also want to make a change in the products offered, saying that in the beginning we are going to have two ovens per product, one in the day and in the afternoon, and that the system will be first-come, first-served.

ChatGPT output:

Sure, here's a sample message that you can use to announce this change:

"Dear valued customers,

We are excited to announce that we are making a change to our bakery operations to better serve you! Starting next week, we will be introducing a new first-come, first-served system for our products. We will have two ovens per product, one in the day and one in the afternoon.

This change will allow us to provide you with fresh products throughout the day and ensure that everyone has an opportunity to enjoy our delicious baked goods. We believe that this new system will improve our service and give you a better experience.

We appreciate your patience and understanding during this transition, and we hope to see you soon at 1, 2, 3 Bakeree to enjoy our freshly baked products.

Thank you for your continued support!

Best regards,

[Your Name/Your Bakery]"

Responding to Reviews

- Prompt: I have just received a review from a client saying that they would love it if we had more options. However, since we are beginning our operation, this is currently not viable, since too many expenses would be involved. We would rather work with a limited amount of products than see what was unsold go to waste. How can I tell this to the client politely without explicitly saying that, for the time being, we are not going to increase our product offering?

ChatGPT output:

Here's a sample response that you can use to address the customer's feedback in a polite and professional manner:

"Dear [Customer's Name],

Thank you for taking the time to share your feedback with us. We appreciate your suggestion for additional menu options, and we are constantly looking for ways to improve our service and offerings.

However, as a new business, we are currently focused on providing the highest quality and freshest products to our customers. While we understand that a wider range of options can be appealing, we believe in offering a limited selection of products that we can guarantee are always fresh and delicious.

We hope that you will continue to enjoy our current offerings, and we welcome any additional feedback or suggestions you may have. Thank you for your support, and we look forward to serving you again soon.

Best regards,

[Your Name/Your Bakery]"

HUMAN RESOURCES AND RECRUITMENT

If you are not planning to bake and tend to the public at the same time, it is likely that you will need some help. Let's suppose that you are going to advertise for the position of a baker and a baker's assistant. ChatGPT can also help you in writing the job requirements, indicating what are the questions you should ask in the interview, and even assess their CV. Let's take a look at what this would look like.

Writing Job Ads

- Prompt: I am looking for an experienced baker that has experience with the products that 1, 2, 3 Bakeree will work with. Can you give me an example of a job advertisement I could post with the needed skills and requirements for the job?

ChatGPT output:

Sure, here's an example of a job advertisement you could use:

Job Title: Experienced Baker

Job Description:

1, 2, 3 Bakeree is looking for an experienced baker to join our team. The successful candidate will be responsible for preparing and baking a variety of sweet and salty products, including normal and gluten-free options. We are seeking a highly skilled individual who can help us maintain the quality and consistency of our products. The candidate must have experience in baking, mixing ingredients, decorating products, and operating bakery equipment.

Responsibilities:

- Prepare and bake a variety of sweet and salty products, including normal and gluten-free options.
- Mix ingredients and ensure consistency of products.

- Decorate products with precision and attention to detail.
- Operate bakery equipment, such as mixers, ovens, and dough sheeters.
- Maintain cleanliness and orderliness of the bakery and equipment.
- Ensure that all products are prepared according to food safety and quality standards.

Requirements:

- At least 3 years of experience as a baker in a commercial bakery setting.
- Experience with normal and gluten-free baking.
- Knowledge of bakery equipment and baking techniques.
- Ability to follow recipes and specifications accurately.
- Attention to detail and commitment to quality.
- Excellent communication and teamwork skills.
- High school diploma or equivalent.

If you are a passionate baker with the skills and experience we are looking for, please send your resume and cover letter to We look forward to hearing from you!

- Prompt 2: And what about for the baker's assistant?

ChatGPT output:

Job Title: Baker's Assistant

Job Description:

We are seeking a skilled and enthusiastic baker's assistant to join our team at 1, 2, 3 Bakeree. As the baker's assistant, you will work closely with the head baker to produce high-quality baked goods for our customers. Your responsibilities will include measuring and mixing ingredients, preparing baking equipment and tools, and assisting with various tasks around the bakery.

Requirements:

- Previous experience working in a bakery or similar setting
- Knowledge of baking techniques and ingredients
- Ability to follow recipes and instructions precisely
- Attention to detail and a commitment to quality
- Ability to work well in a fast-paced environment

- Excellent communication and teamwork skills
- Flexibility to work early mornings, weekends, and holidays as needed

If you are passionate about baking and are looking for a challenging and rewarding opportunity, we encourage you to apply for this position. Please send your resume and a cover letter to [insert contact information].

Coming Up With Interview Questions

- Prompt: What are some interview questions I can ask the candidate for the baker position regarding soft and hard skills? Give me 10 examples.

ChatGPT output:

Soft Skills:

1. How do you handle pressure and stress in a fast-paced work environment?
2. How do you manage your time effectively to meet production goals and deadlines?
3. Can you describe your communication style when working in a team environment?
4. How do you handle constructive feedback from managers or colleagues?

5. Have you ever had to deal with a difficult customer, and how did you handle the situation?

Hard Skills:

1. How do you adjust recipes for different batch sizes?
2. Can you walk me through the baking process for a croissant?
3. How do you troubleshoot common baking issues, such as under or over-proofing?
4. Can you demonstrate your knowledge of gluten-free baking techniques and ingredients?
5. How do you maintain a clean and organized work environment to ensure food safety and quality?

Writing Candidate Outreach Emails

- Prompt: I have received over 10 resumes to evaluate, but I am only going to select the top three for an interview because they seem a better fit according to the characteristics you gave me. What is an example of a message I can send to those who will not be considered?

ChatGPT output:

Dear [Applicant's Name],

Thank you for applying to [Position] at 1, 2, 3 Bakeree. We appreciate your interest in our bakery and the time you took to submit your application.

After reviewing your qualifications and experience, we have decided to move forward with other candidates who are better aligned with the requirements of the position. Please understand that our decision was not a reflection of your abilities or potential as a baker.

We would like to thank you once again for considering us in your job search and wish you the best of luck in your future endeavors.

Sincerely,

[Your Name]

Assessing Candidates

- Prompt: What are the qualities that I should look for when hiring a baker for 1 , 2, 3 Bakeree and how should I assess the candidates? Provide me with an overview in bullet points separating soft and hard skills. Also indicate if I should carry out a tasting test.

ChatGPT output:

Here are some qualities you can look for in a baker and ways to assess them during the interview process:

Soft Skills:

- Attention to detail
- Ability to work in a fast-paced environment
- Strong work ethic and reliability
- Good communication skills to work with other staff members
- Passion for baking and interest in learning new techniques
- Ability to work in a team environment

Hard Skills:

- Knowledge of baking techniques and methods
- Ability to mix, shape, and bake a variety of baked goods, including bread, pastries, and cakes
- Familiarity with ingredient measurements and recipe scaling
- Ability to maintain a clean and organized workspace
- Familiarity with food safety and sanitation regulations

To assess these skills, you can:

- Review their resume and application for relevant experience and education
- Ask about their previous baking experience and what skills they gained from it
- Inquire about their knowledge of baking techniques and ingredient measurements
- Request a demonstration of their baking skills, either in-person or through a video submission
- Conduct reference checks with previous employers or colleagues

Regarding the tasting test, it could be a good idea to ask candidates to bring in samples of their baked goods, but keep in mind that this may not always be feasible or necessary, especially if their skills and experience are strong enough to speak for themselves.

ACCOUNTING AND FINANCE

Lastly, when speaking about a business, there is specific accounting and financial information that you need to know. However, if you have never worked in the area or started a business of your own, you might need guidance on how to work out these matters. Here, I want to reinforce that ChatGPT will not replace a formal accountant or financial advisor, but it can be used to obtain more information and details regarding what they are telling you.

Giving Tax Advice

- Prompt: What are the taxes that I should add to the products I sell in 1, 2, 3 Bakeree?

ChatGPT output:

The taxes that you should add to the products you sell in 1, 2, 3 Bakeree will depend on the tax laws in your location. In general, bakeries may be subject to sales tax, which is a tax on the sale of goods and services. The sales tax rate may vary depending on the state or local jurisdiction in which your business is located. You may also need to pay other taxes, such as income tax or property tax, depending on your business structure and other factors.

To ensure that you are following the appropriate tax laws and regulations, it is recommended that you consult with a local tax professional or accountant who can provide you with specific guidance based on your location and business needs.

- Prompt 2: What are the taxes that my business will need to pay to operate that I should consider adding to the cost of the product? The baker will be located in Ontario, Canada.

ChatGPT output:

As a business operating in Ontario, Canada, there are several taxes that you will need to consider when determining your costs and pricing strategy. Here are some of the key taxes:

1. Harmonized Sales Tax (HST): HST is a combination of the federal Goods and Services Tax (GST) and the provincial sales tax (PST). In Ontario, the HST rate is currently 13%. You will need to register for an HST account and collect and remit the HST on taxable sales.

2. Corporate Income Tax (CIT): As a corporation, you will be required to pay corporate income tax on your taxable income. The federal rate is currently 15%, and the provincial rate in Ontario is currently 12.5%.

3. Payroll Taxes: If you have employees, you will need to deduct and remit payroll taxes, including Canada Pension Plan (CPP) contributions, Employment Insurance (EI) premiums, and income tax.

4. Property Taxes: If you own or lease property, you will need to pay property taxes to the municipality where the property is located.

It is important to consult with a tax professional or accountant to ensure that you are complying with all tax requirements and accurately calculating your tax liabilities.

Company's Financial Performance

- Prompt: I have been making approximately $250.00 per day with 1, 2, 3, Bakeree. I pay the baker a wage of $2,500 before tax and $1,500 to the assistant before tax in Ontario, Canada. My costs are usually around $3,000 monthly. How would you evaluate my financial performance? Is there anything I need to change?

ChatGPT output:

Based on the information provided, there seems to be a discrepancy between the daily revenue and the monthly costs. If the daily revenue is $250, then the monthly revenue would be around $7,500. However, if the monthly costs are $3,000, then the net profit would be around $4,500.

Paying the baker and assistant a total of $4,000 per month before tax would leave only $500 for other expenses such as rent, ingredients, and utilities. This could be challenging to sustain in the long term.

Therefore, some changes that could be made to improve financial performance include:

- Increasing prices of products to increase revenue
- Reviewing and reducing costs wherever possible
- Considering expanding product offerings to increase revenue
- Evaluating and potentially adjusting wages for the baker and assistant to ensure they are being compensated fairly while also considering the financial viability of the business.

It may also be helpful to consult with a financial advisor or accountant to ensure the financial health of the business and to develop a plan for sustainable growth.

Financial Projection Generation

- Prompt: Can you make a financial projection based on the previously given information and considering the previously given information and that: the months of June to August are the busiest during the weekend, where I earn approximately $500.00 per day on sales. The slowest months are December to February, when the income is $190.00 per day including weekends.

ChatGPT output:

Certainly! Based on the information you provided, here is a financial projection for the next year:

- Average daily revenue: $250
- Average monthly revenue: $7,500 ($250 x 30 days)
- Annual revenue (excluding June to August and December to February): $67,500 ($7,500 x 9 months)
- Annual revenue (including June to August): $120,000 (($7,500 x 9 months) + ($500 x 90 days))
- Annual revenue (including June to August and December to February): $130,350 (($7,500 x 9 months) + ($500 x 90 days) + ($190 x 75 days))
- Annual costs: $36,000 ($3,000 x 12 months)
- Annual wage expenses (before tax): $45,000 (($2,500 + $1,500) x 12 months)

- Annual net income (excluding June to August and December to February): $26,500 ($67,500 - $36,000 - $45,000)
- Annual net income (including June to August): $79,500 ($120,000 - $36,000 - $45,000)
- Annual net income (including June to August and December to February): $70,850 ($130,350 - $36,000 - $45,000)

As you can see, your financial performance looks solid, with potential for significant growth during the busiest months. However, it may be worthwhile to consider ways to reduce costs or increase revenue during slower months to improve overall profitability.

Identifying Trends or Patterns

- Prompt: Can you give me an analysis on the trends and patterns of my financial health?

ChatGPT output:

As an AI language model, I do not have access to your actual financial data to conduct an analysis. However, based on the information provided, it appears that your business experiences fluctuations in sales and revenue depending on the time of the year.

The months of June to August are the busiest, where sales are approximately $500.00 per day. On the other hand, the slowest months are December to February, where sales drop to $190.00 per day including weekends.

It's important to consider how to balance the costs during the slower months to ensure that the business stays afloat. Perhaps consider increasing marketing efforts during the slower months to attract more customers or offer promotions to incentivize sales.

Overall, it's important to have a solid financial plan in place to ensure that the business can weather any fluctuations in sales and revenue.

CONSIDERATIONS

As you have seen in this chapter, I have provided you with several different prompt ideas that range from more to less specific so you can analyze ChatGPT's performance. Here, you should note that the language it uses is very similar to a human conversation and that it does not use complicated words and jargon, making it easy for the layperson to understand. Now that you have an idea of the things that the application can do, you can try it out using your own example or even expand on the questions for our fictional business 1, 2,

3 Bakeree by adding more or less details and seeing how it will respond.

In the next chapter, we are going to take a look at other areas in your life where ChatGPT can help you and how you can apply its use. Although I won't be giving you the prompts and outputs as you have seen in this chapter, feel free to use that notebook I mentioned and jot down a few questions. You can even keep your computer open while reading and prompt the application as you read so you can see the information it will provide you with.

7

ENHANCING YOUR PERSONAL LIFE

N ow that you already know how to have ChatGPT help you with your business, how would you feel if I told you a little more about how it can help you in your personal life? As far-fetched as it might seem, the application can also help you for issues that range from finding dating advice to more realistic applications such as helping you with your studies.

However, before I continue, I must make a very important note on what you must **not** use ChatGPT for. This is because there is one thing (or two, for that matter) that the application cannot replace are doctors and therapists. Just when it was launched, some people were using it to give them medical advice and to help them with serious mental health issues. Let me tell you that this is **not** a good idea. While it may be good in analyzing symptoms, getting them right 88% of the time, this still is not 100%, which means that a doctor must be consulted **always** (University of Maryland School of Medicine, 2023). There is no such thing as replacing a physician when talking about your health.

The same goes for mental illnesses. Although ChatGPT might **sound** like they are giving you good advice, you must be careful because it does not understand the subtleties of written language. This means that it will not be able to properly diagnose you and it could lead to serious, life-threatening consequences. Therefore, if you think you need help, you must search for a licensed therapist or a doctor that will be able to help you and identify the appropriate path you need to follow. Because of risks that using ChatGPT might bring you when we talk about health, these are the two areas in which you, once again, should **not** rely on the application.

With this important alert duly given, it is time to take a look into what ChatGPT **can** do for you and what it will help you with. Read on to find out how you can prompt it for enhancing your life.

DATING AND RELATIONSHIP ADVICE

As surprising as this might seem, have you ever thought that if you can "train" ChatGPT with relevant information on a business you might be able to do the same when dating? Sounds weird, but it works. According to Yalalov (2022) he tried adding information on ChatGPT regarding his Tinder profile and, amazingly, they seem to have delivered some very sound advice. The information ranged from how to create a successful profile in the dating app to what pickup lines should be used when talking to someone.

One of the main factors to take into account here is that since it will be using NLP, it will be easier to incorporate its outputs once you start prompting it. And, much like you saw in the case of 1, 2, 3 Bakeree, the more you use ChatGPT for this type of information, the better it will get over time. In addition to this, if you are feeling out of ideas at the moment of where to take your date, you can just input what they like to do and enjoy and ask the application to give you suggestions of where you can take them. How is this for a good problem-solver?

In addition to this, Houghton (2023) carried out a similar experiment with the software, but instead of asking it for improvements on their Tinder account, they were more specific and asked about relationship advice. According to the author, she was surprised with some of the thoughtful answers and the human-like approach it had to the questions that were asked. Some of them included how to break up with someone and what was the most important question that someone could ask on a date.

Based on the prompt and the output that the application gave, she was pretty satisfied that it could help break the ice or start conversations if a date starts to get boring. I know that I have made you curious, but I won't spoil the fun. If you still have your computer open, try prompting ChatGPT for some dating or relationship advice. I can assure you that you will be surprised with how much common sense it has and the quality of the answers you will find!

IMPROVE YOUR WRITING

In the same way that you can train ChatGPT to think like your business persona, you can do the same to make it mimic the writing of someone else or even improve your writing. Let's suppose that you are working on a blog article but you are not finding it interesting or entertaining enough. One of the possibilities you have is to ask it to write imitating the style of someone else, or even just prompt it by telling it why you think your text is not interesting and what you would like to be added to it to change this. As an example, try writing a simple story without any emotion and prompt ChatGPT to make it more exciting and see the result you will have.

In addition to this, if you are writing the same article and have no time to edit your work or to find someone to do it for you, you can use the application to do it for you. All you will need to do is input the text you wrote and ask ChatGPT to correct spelling and grammar, press enter, and you will immediately have the results. You can do this for your personal communication, work content, and any other texts that you are writing. Therefore, use the software as a means to improve your writing (you can even ask it to point out what you did wrong as a manner of feedback) and enhance your communication.

HELPING WITH STUDIES

Are you having trouble understanding the content of that physics class that you had today? Well, one of the advantages of ChatGPT is that it can help you study complex subjects and summarize information. This means that if you have a doubt regarding a specific theme, you can prompt the tool to explain it to you in a way that you will understand. If you remember that it uses NLP, this will make it all the more advantageous, since it will bring the concept to you without using too much jargon and technical language.

If you need the information to be processed to the minimum, you can also prompt it "to explain it to a six-year-old," and it will do so in even simpler terms. The same can be said for articles that you are finding too complex or do not have enough time to read. You can feed it the information and it will bring you a comprehensive summary in a language you can understand and make conclusions. Once again may I remind you that since this is a tool that has a learning algorithm, the more information you give it on a subject, the more it will be able to help and explain things to you.

As a last tip on using ChatGPT for your studies, you can also prompt it to help you prepare for tests and exams. By requesting that it comes up with different questions on a subject, you can test your knowledge and see how much you still need to study. In addition to this, you can also ask it to correct the answers that you give to the questions that it asks you. How is that for a personal tutor? Using this will help you save time and prepare for tests on various subjects and classes.

On the other hand, I do not suggest using ChatGPT as a research tool or to help you complete your homework for two simple reasons. The first is that the information, as you already know, might not be accurate and by prompting it you could be missing out on the most relevant and updated information on the subject. The second is because the tool is known to lie and make up information, which can end up putting you in a difficult position with your teacher.

Even if you do prompt it for writing a certain paper and then use a search engine to find results and verify its accuracy, I would say that it will just mean that you are doing the work twice, wouldn't you agree? Therefore, although it might sound tempting to do so, you might want to stay away from ChatGPT for your school activities. One last thing to consider is that your teacher probably can recognize how their students write and, therefore, seeing a text that is grammatically perfect and that presents perfect logic might make them suspicious that you wrote it with the help of AI and can get you in serious trouble.

CREATE DIET PLANS AND RECIPES

Although I did say that ChatGPT cannot replace a physician, creating a diet plan is possibly the only situation in which this is partially acceptable. When I say partially it is because even if you are able to create a dietary plan for yourself by using the tool, it is important that you get the opinion of a certified nutritionist to ensure that you are not missing out on any important vitamins in the plan. On the other hand, if you are in a situation in which the doctor gives you a list of things you are allowed to eat, then it won't hurt to input this in the tool and ask it to build you a weekly meal plan adjusted to the orientation. In these cases, you will see that ChatGPT will prove to be effective and provide you with more alternatives than you can imagine.

What is even better is that you can also use the tool to help you create different dishes and recipes based on the ingredients you have at home. This means that no more will you start cooking and need to run to the store to buy that extra item that you are missing. If you are looking for creative alternatives, all you need to do is prompt ChatGPT with what you have in your pantry and refrigerator and ask it to prepare a meal based on what is available. Not only is this a good resource for you to use that old can of beans that you bought some time ago and don't know what dish to make with it, but it will also help you optimize what you already have by avoiding waste.

Lastly, I want you to consider the advantages of having ChatGPT prepare you with a weekly menu **and** tell you what you need to buy for that week. No more going to the supermarket and randomly buying things that you do not know if you will use or not. By establishing a creative meal plan for you and your family, you can buy only the products that you will use for those meals, helping you save money and avoid the risk of having the products expire without use.

FINDING WAYS TO MAKE MONEY

We all have different abilities and talents. However, if you are unsure of what you can do to earn money with these, ChatGPT will be able to help you. By feeding it information on what you are capable of doing and what your strong points are, it will give you a list of activities that can help you start a business or earn money. Although they might not all be right for you, there is certainly something that you will find that will make you excited.

In addition to this, it does not need to be only about what you are good at, but also refers to the ideas you have and if they are worth pursuing. You can ask ChatGPT to help you brainstorm business ideas and different ways to make an extra income by telling it the activities that you like to do. And it does not matter how different these things are or that they are relevant in distinct areas, the important thing is to prompt it with the largest amount of information possible so it can bring you the best results.

If you are near your computer, why don't you try it now. First, prompt ChatGPT by telling it that you want some ideas that will help you make money based on your abilities and interests. Next, write a list with ten items of the things that you like to do the most and another list with the ten things you think you are good at and feed it to the application. You will be amazed at the results it will bring you and, who knows, it might be the start of a new endeavor in your life!

PART IV

ENVISIONING THE FUTURE

8

LATEST DEVELOPMENTS IN CHATBOT TECHNOLOGY

There is no doubt that, with the release of ChatGPT, there has been a shift in the way society sees chatbots. The transformation that the application has brought to our society seems to be endless with all of its uses and features. As you will see in this chapter, technology companies are now racing to ensure that they provide the public with the best solutions to fight off what ChatGPT has started. Even some of the most recent investments made in the before-attractive metaverse are being shut down to focus on AI development.

Despite this, AI and machine learning are still matters that we need to look into and study further—there is no way that we can fully comprehend its full capacity and potential. Look at what happened with the AI that

Facebook was developing: The computers started developing a language of their own, that was incomprehensible to humans, and the project had to be shut down (Baraniuk, 2017). Although the story captivated the media's attention due to its tabloid approach, much of what happened is still unknown. Baraniuk (2017) states that, "A better explanation is that the neural networks were simply trying to modify human language for the purposes of more successful interactions—whether their approach worked or not was another matter."

But is this possible? Well, I guess it will depend on the quantity of sci-fi movies you have watched and how much you trust the learning algorithm to work. It is, nevertheless, astounding what these machines can do and how they can interpret our language and understand what we are trying to say. On the other hand, you should remember that chatbots do not have or understand the concept of feeling and that it uses word prompt identification techniques to come up with the best alternatives. While this means that it is unlikely that we will soon have a robot acting like a villain we see in the movies, it also makes them incredibly dangerous as AI-oriented weapons (Baraniuk, 2017).

Weapons may likely not identify children and other vulnerable groups to attack, or might not have the sensitivity to do so. Despite that, if AI still starts developing its own language and start threatening human existence, which is highly unlikely as Kucera (2017) mentions, there is a simple solution: pull the plug. Essentially speaking, "Shutting down a chatbot when it stops showing a reasonable outcome is about as ominous as changing a faulty light bulb" (Kucera, 2017).

This, however, does not mean that AI is not changing or that it is not going to change the way our society works. It is very probable, from the shifts that we have been witnessing big and small technology companies make, that we are entering a new age of "AI race," in which each of them is trying to overcome the other. The competition is set to determine who develops the best technology and increase market releases in the near future. Let's explore this a little more and see what is going on in the market and how the future of AI is being shaped by the release of ChatGPT.

HOW CHATGPT IS IMPACTING THE FUTURE OF AI

According to Chow and Perrigo (2023), the development of AI chatbots have had a similar "breakthrough" impact in society as the invention of social media. According to the authors, the main indicator of this disruption can be seen with the ChatGPT having reached 100 million users in only one month. In a small comparison to some of the most popular applications, such as TikTok and Facebook, the application took less than one-fourth of the time to reach this incredible number of users—"it took TikTok nine months and Instagram over two years to reach the same user milestone" (Ivancie, 2023).

These numbers only show the impressive rate by which AI is growing in the market. Although these numbers refer to users and might oscillate as the tool becomes less of a novelty, the numbers when we consider technology companies are not different—in fact, they are even more astonishing. According to Nduka (2023), here are a few numbers that are certain to leave you impressed with how much Ai is being invested in:

- Apple has bought more than 25 startup companies that are related to AI development since 2010. The number is followed by Google, which has done the same for 15 companies within the same area of expertise.
- The amount invested in companies that are working with developing AI tools reached almost $40 billion in the first semester of 2021 and is expected to reach the $50 trillion house by 2023.

- There was an amazing increase of 270% in the number of businesses using AI between the years of 2015 and 2019, and this number is likely to increase with the introduction of ChatGPT in the market and the new "AI arms race" that companies are engaging in.
- AI has become so significant to companies and a synonym of evolution and success that 4 out of every 5 consider investing in the AI business and consider it a business priority.
- Company managers believe that AI tools can help employees produce more and more than 85% of the credit for the future success of the business to the evolving AI tools that are appearing in the market.

As you can see, AI has the potential to become a very powerful tool that will help determine the next steps in our relationship with technology. "It is exactly this immense power that makes the current moment so electrifying—and so dangerous" (Baraniuk, 2017). To have a better idea of how this will be done, read along and see what are the possible integrations that are already being made with different online platforms.

CHATGPT INTEGRATION WITH OTHER PLATFORMS

The promise of a revolution with ChatGPT not only started when it provided users with human-like answers to questions but also with the potential that it has to integrate with other online platforms. Differently from what we saw in Chapter 4, where we talked about plugins that provided the user with non-native features of the software, there is also the possibility of integrating the AI tool to other applications.

Even though this integration is possible, you will need to have some idea of Python coding to carry it out. On the bright side, you will be able to connect to Slack, Facebook Messenger, Salesforce, Microsoft Teams, Telegram, WhatsApp, and many more applications by just accessing their code library (Gabe A, (M.S.), 2023). According to the author, this can be done in four simple steps,

1. Select the application you want to integrate ChatGPT to from the list of available platforms.
2. If you don't have an account in the tool that you have selected, you must create one according to your need—personal or professional.
3. Connect the application of your choice to ChatGPT.

4. Personalize the messages you want to send.

And that's it! Even if you feel like you will not be able to do this on your own, you must remember that you can use the AI tool to help you integrate it or have a professional developer help you. By doing this, you will be able to feed ChatGPT with the specific information you want it to react to and train it to give the responses according to your needs. Once again, let me remind you that all this information is stored in the application's database, so be careful with what you choose to upload!

The list of applications you can integrate ChatGPT to range from social media to Excel sheets and all that is in between. Here is a list of 15 examples where this can be applied (*ChatGPT Integrations in 2023*, 2023):

- Microsoft Excel
- Google Slides
- Facebook Messenger
- Google Business Profile
- Discord
- Spotify
- Dropbox
- Azure OpenAI Service
- Simple Texting
- Code Assist

- Microsoft Teams
- LinkedIn
- GitLab
- Google Analytics
- Zoom
- Zapier

Apart from these, there are several others that you will be able to connect with, but I want to take a moment here and talk about ChatGPT's integration with Zapier. The main reason for this aside is that when you connect the application to the Zapier ChatGPT plugin, you will be able to access thousands of other applications without needing to connect them one by one. Therefore, this means that you can use one connection—the one with Zapier—to connect your most used platforms in one place without needing to change anything! According to the company, "You can ask ChatGPT to execute any of Zapier's 50,000 actions (including search, update, and write) with Zapier's 5,000+ supported apps, turning chat into action. It can write an email, then send it for you" (Alston, 2023).

PROMISING INVESTMENTS IN THE AI RACE

But what are these companies investing in and what can I expect of the future developments of AI? That, dear reader, is a very good question. In this final section of the chapter, I have separated three different advances that have been happening so far that have been made public, of which one has already been released: ChatGPT 4. Yes! Although it is still in an early assessment phase and can only be used by paying a subscription, the newer version of the application seems to increase the lead that Microsoft already has in the market. Here is an overview of the most commented applications that are being developed.

ChatGPT 4

Released to the public in March, 2023, the newer version of ChatGPT4 is limited for users who subscribe to the application, on the contrary of ChatGPT 3.5, which is the free version that anyone can use and that this book is based on. According to the demonstration presented by OpenAI, the improved version of the chatbot has features that include even the possibility to upload images, enabling the user to analyze pictures and even build websites from a simple drawing.

In addition to this, according to what was shown, it is possible to have more precise responses from the application, including having it understand better the human sense of humor. This means that, in the long run, it is possible that the users of the platform will have an even better experience in finding answers to the prompts they feed the tool. One of the improvements is that it will be able to analyze 25,000 words rather than the 4,000 that ChatGPT 3.5 currently enables the user to prompt per use.

In an important new feature, you remember when I mentioned that ChatGPT was limited in resources because the information it was trained on was limited to 2021? Well, in this new version of Chat GPT, you can just prompt it with a link to an internet page and it will be able to "read" the information and bring you a summary of what it contains. One of the places that you will be able to see this feature at work, if you do not want or plan to subscribe to it, is in Bing Chat, the enhanced version of the Microsoft search engine. In another enhancement, the responses that it will provide the user are said to be considerably safer than the previous version, disabling content that may be damaging or bringing more factual responses.

Finally, ChatGPT4 will be able to read and understand codes in all languages, which will enable you to create or mimic the programming of certain games and pages just by prompting it. In addition to this, it is better in responding tests, having passed with flying colors exams applied to students such as the bar exams, performing among the top ranked exam-takers, compared to its previous version, when it ranked among the lowest scorers.

And the tendency is that the tools get even more sophisticated in the future. Microsoft has confirmed that it will increase its partnership with OpenAI and will invest an additional $10 billion in the company so it can continue its research and AI development (Q.ai, 2023). The idea is that the company integrates AI even more into its resources and services, jumping ahead of several of its competitors that are still struggling with their own AI initiatives, as we will now see.

Google Bard

As you have probably done, several users are replacing search engines by prompting ChatGPT to answer their questions. Because of this, "Google's management even declared a 'code red' as there are concerns that the chatbot could replace search engines" (Q.ai, 2023). This means that Alphabet, the company that owns Google, needs to start investing in AI tools, and fast, if it does not want to be permanently replaced, especially since most of the company's revenues come from advertisements when searches are carried out. In addition to this, it doesn't help that its main (although far-behind) competitor, Bing, is already incorporating ChatGPT's features into its capabilities.

Although it has been focusing its sights toward the AI market, most specialists say that it is undeniable that Microsoft has started leading and still leads the race among big tech companies (Kharpal, 2023). According to specialist Richard Kramer, heard by Kharpal (2023), "Google's issue is that they have the brightest minds in AI, they have the rockstars, they have a third of the top hundred cited papers in AI, but they're an engineering-led company, and they have not productized what they've done." These efforts have left the tech giant to create what is being called "Apprentice Bard."

According to Elias (2023), "Apprentice Bard looks similar to ChatGPT: Employees can enter a question in a dialog box and get a text answer, then give feedback on the response." It is safe to say, however, that whatever Alphabet plans to do, incorporating AI into the world's most used search engine could lead to a revolution. The fact is that it will have to run after the progress that ChatGPT has made so far and the promise of what ChatGPT promises to deliver. Mathur (2023) says that "One of the key factors differentiating Bard from ChatGPT is the former's ability to respond based on current data, staying up-to-date with news and trends. The bot cited data from as recently as January 2023 during internal testing," although we have already seen that ChatGPT4 has overcome this problem with the link input.

Regarding the other differences between both of the chatbots, Leong and Martindale (2023) say that:

> But there are a couple of minor differences in feature sets. Google Bard lets you give prompts via voice using your device's microphone, which is neat for a hands-free experience. It also offers a quick "Google it" button which gives you in-line links to continue research outside of Bard. One other neat feature of Bard is "drafts." Each time you enter a prompt and start a conversation with Bard, it'll offer you different drafts, or variations of responses. It's a convenient way to pick through a few different options to hone in on what you're aiming for. I also like the way Bard displays previous prompts. Click on "Bard activity," and you'll see each of your prompts, which you can see details or delete from history. You can also turn off Bard storing your activity (para 12).

Safe to say that the "war" between both companies is far from over. In addition to this, there is yet another company that you should keep your eye out for. Can you guess what it is? If you guessed Meta, Facebook's owner, then you are more than correct.

Facebook Blenderbot

In the beginning of March 2023, the technology market was taken by surprise with the announcement made by Meta that it was leaving its metaverse project aside to focus on pursuing AI. The tech giant, which had been spending over $1 billion in creating its virtual reality space, was even renamed to mirror the shift in focus—thys name Meta (Leffer, 2023). It has since started investing more money in the Facebook Artificial Intelligence Research group (FAIR) since working on improving "BlenderBot3," the company's chatbot.

The first reviews of the application, in late 2022, ranked it from bad to worse. Among being inaccurate, it was also shown to provide fake information or, in other words, lie. In one review written by Piper (2022), she claims that "There are a lot of different ways to measure the performance of a chatbot. By nearly any of them, Blenderbot is really, really bad." And this was only one of the many reviews in which the users claimed to have a negative experience with the AI tool. In another review written by DeGeurin (2022), they claim that "Shockingly, it turns out Meta's bot actually isn't racist (yet, at least). In fact, it *really, really* wants you to know how totally not racist it is."

The reviews, if you search the internet, will vary although they will mostly be negative. Most of the people who tested BlenderBot claim that its information does not seem to mimic at all human communication when compared to other tools and that it is highly unreliable. It is safe to say that, based on the overall opinion of those who reviewed the tool, there is still a lot the company has to do to improve their chatbot if they want to compete with larger companies.

However, as we think about the implications that advanced AI will have in the market and in our lives, an important question must be asked: *Will AI eventually replace humans?* That is a very good question. And, as we reach the last chapter of this book, I invite you to join me in reflecting about the subject and learn what are specialists' and my opinions on the subject. In addition to this, we are also going to look at some of the ongoing impacts of technology in several areas, which will make us certain about one thing: The technology world as we know it is on the brink of change.

9

WILL AI REPLACE HUMANS?

Success in creating effective AI, could be the biggest event in the history of our civilization. Or the worst. We just don't know. So we cannot know if we will be infinitely helped by AI, or ignored by it and side-lined, or conceivably destroyed by it.

— STEPHEN HAWKING

The world-famous physicist said this in 2017 — roughly five years before the first chatbot was released. Although he mentioned the positive aspects that AI could bring to humanity, the damage that it could make was not forgotten. Among the threats, he named the potential use of AI in weapons that could be used by more powerful nations to control others that were smaller and the potential effect it could have on the global economy (Kharpal, 2017).

If we use this last chapter of the book to reflect upon the advantages and disadvantages that AI can bring, the balance is unclear. While more powerful countries could use this to increase the technology of their military, it could also bring a huge improvement to some of the things that we do today. Duggal (2023) says that for a few companies, being available 24 hours, seven days a week can be an advantage—companies might be able to be productive throughout the whole day, without pauses, and answer to customer demands at any time of the day. In addition to this, it would enable a save in costs for its general operation.

Another advantage of using AI would be to reduce the risks on both operations and on difficult situations that could threaten human life. If you consider several tasks that are being carried out by humans, some of them could easily be replaced by a machine to avoid physical and mental problems. This brings us to another positive aspect of AI, which is to eliminate the need of people carrying out repetitive tasks that do not challenge them. This could mean that new paths will open for different careers and approaches in how people carry out their lives, without the need to perform tasks that a robot could easily do.

Finally, if we consider the advantages of AI, one of the most important that can be mentioned is the elimination of human error. No matter what field we are talking about—from engineering to science—their use of AI applications can reduce the chances of mistakes being made due to mistakes. It can aid engineers with calculations for constructions, help doctors and nurses with patient care and monitoring, and perform tests in software development. What I am trying to say is that, if guided properly, AI can be a huge advantage for several areas that might need more precision or that are lacking qualified professionals simply because it is not attractive.

But, as I mentioned earlier, there are the problems that AI brings that can be more common than weaponizing technology. Remember how I said that students are using ChatGPT to do their homework? This is just one of the simplest of the forms by which AI can pose a danger. This means that we are using our brains less for things that we should learn that are taught in school and more for learning how to prompt a machine. Examples of where this could be clearly prejudicial are when a student needs to practice their creative side or if they need to carry out critical thinking.

Still thinking about the disadvantages that AI has I could also mention things such as the lack of feelings and expression on what is used, the potential of using bias in the answers, the lack of confirmation that the information is in fact, true, and the limitation in understanding ethical and morality matters that are so important in human relationships. However, just as Stephen Hawking mentioned, one of the largest dangers lies in the economy—what will happen if AI starts replacing people and taking over jobs?

As you have seen in the beginning of this book, several companies are already using AI for specific tasks and people are losing their jobs. In addition to this, there are several areas that will be threatened if AI continues to evolve. In one clear example, I could name voice-scrapping in the internet to use people's voices in videos and narrations without their authorization. Rest assured that if it is someone famous, it will likely be identified. But what about if we are talking about a common narrator who lives off this occupation and suddenly starts losing jobs because AI is being used? What will happen to people that are in these situations? This leads me to the question that I want us to think about: *Will AI replace humans?*

WHY AI CAN'T REPLACE HUMANS—FOR NOW

My first answer to the question above would be that no, AI is not capable of replacing humans... At least for now. It still does not possess the emotional intelligence of a human to be capable of dealing with difficult situations (Oluwaniyi, 2023). To illustrate this, I want you to think about a few examples.

Let's suppose that you work in the client relationship service of a company and a client calls with demands and complains about a product. AI is still not able to empathize with the person to the point where it will listen and help them calm down. Most likely, by using its rational approach and lack of emotions, it will make the client even more nervous, since it will not be able to understand the customer's frustration or irritation. "Smart business owners and company executives understand the importance of appealing to the emotions of staff and clients. A machine can't achieve such levels of human connection, while, as a human, there are ways to increase your emotional intelligence" (Oluwaniyi, 2023).

In another example we could talk about physicians. Determining the illness of a patient depends on several factors, one of which is talking to them and being able to ask the right questions based on the information they provide you with. In addition to this, sometimes physical examination is needed and even the study of the patients features as they describe what they are feeling. And we are only talking about medical doctors and not mentioning psychologists, for example. If you think about the importance that relating to the other's emotions has for these professionals, it makes it hard to believe that it would be possible to replace them.

Now, I want you to remember what I mentioned about needing to check the information that chatbots give you. This means that even if you are using ChatGPT, for example to carry out research, you will still need to verify the information that it is giving you to ensure accuracy. This means that even if the application does the research work for you, it will be essential to check and see if what it is saying is correct—remember, chatbots are able to lie, we have already seen this!

In addition to this, I think that there is no AI without human input. Humans are the ones who create the machines. They are the ones who determine what the machine is supposed to do and how they are supposed to work. It is based on the data that we feed them with that they will generate their outputs, or logical responses (Gupta, 2023b). Their lack of ability to think creatively is something that **might** not change, since this is a human ability. It is possible that it can learn to improvise, but to think according to reactions and situations without previous input from a human is almost impossible. Machines need humans to give them, for the lack of a better word, parameters.

If you are still unsure about this, I propose a challenge. I want to prompt ChatGPT to write a novel for you. It can be regarding any genre you prefer, but let's think about one with emotions. Ask it to write you a love story that contains the elements of love, suffering, betrayal, and forgiveness. As a result, you will probably see a well-written, but emotionally "cold" story. The story might give you a sense of sentiment, but I doubt that it will give you the depth and nuances that a human author is able to.

Am I saying that we are irreplaceable? Well, yes, but also no. It is possible that some jobs will be replaced by AI tools. But this does not mean that **everything** will. It is just the evolution of technology that will take over some activities, create others, and some will remain the same. Think about some years ago, before photo-printing machines. We used to take our film rolls to a developing store where the employees would manually "print" the pictures. With the arrival of these machines, this is a practically extinct profession. Those who used to work with this lost their jobs over time because technology took over. They might have changed or adapted

their careers, who knows? The point here is that technology led to a change, and people were forced to
adapt. The same is likely to happen with AI—at least
for now.

THE RISE OF GENERATIVE AI

We have already looked at how AI applications, such as
ChatGPT, uses the inputs that are given to it to
generate responses. However, before we finish off, it is
important to mention the concept of generative AI, or
Gen-AI. Differently from the traditional AI tools that
classify, analyze, and research the data that it contains
in their databases, Gen-AI is a branch of AI where
things are created or, in other words, generated. If you
are right now thinking: *Then if ChatGPT is a tool that can
write an original story, it is also a Gen-AI tool!* If that was
the conclusion you reached, then congratulations, you
are more than correct!

Eliaçik (2023) puts it in a very simple definition to
understand, where Gen-AI is referred to as,

> The technology that allows the generation of
> new content using pre-existing text, audio files,
> or images is known as generative artificial intel-
> ligence (AI). Through the use of generative artifi-
> cial intelligence, computers are able to recognize

the underlying pattern associated with the input
and generate equivalent content (para. 4).

This means, for example, if we look back at Chapter 6,
when we created content for our 1, 2, 3 Bakeree
project, we were essentially using Gen-AI to create the
information that was going to be given to the public,
especially when we were writing the marketing
content. If you think this is amazing, you must
consider how this will impact human creation in
general. If you remember that ChatGPT4 is able to
recognize drawings and, from these, establish a design,
it might not be that hard to understand what I'm
getting at.

"Every sector that relies on humans to produce original
work, such as social media and gaming, advertising and
architecture, coding and graphic design, product design
and law, and marketing and sales, is ripe for innovation" (Eliaçik, 2023). Therefore, you can only imagine
with a few ideas what these tools will be able to do. And
if you think that we are still far away from reaching this
point in the development of AI, then let me be the first
to tell you that it already exists and it is only getting
better!

If you still have doubts and questions, I will now show
you how and where Gen-AI is already being used (or

could be used)—and be ready, because this might surprise you!

Generative Art

One of the places in which Gen-AI is generating the most comments is in the art scenery. This is because some models use examples and drawings from other artists to create what is "unique" art. However, this poses a challenge since there are royalties and copyright issues. For example, you can upload the drawings of your favorite artist and have AI create an image for you using the same traits. The same way, you can also take a picture and ask AI to transform it into a Van Gogh look-alike with the same paint brush stroke characteristics.

On the other hand, it is also possible to create images based on a text description that you have from an image. AI will read the text, interpret it, and make a drawing based on what you have requested. However, you must remember to be as detailed as possible since the art will be based on the description that you provide it.

Writing

As you have seen with ChatGPT, creating original texts is possible and already a reality with AI. Based on the information you provide, the application will create different types of texts based on the knowledge it has and what it has "learned." Although some of what it may produce can be considered "dry" and "emotion-less," it helps to know that you can edit it to best suit your needs and demands.

It is possible that, throughout time, the Gen-AI tools for writing will become more elaborated and be capable of creating texts with more feeling but, as of now, this is not something that it does. At the same time, it is important to remember the limitations that some AI tools have and that it might not necessarily be giving you accurate information regarding the topic that you want. Therefore, it is always good to carry out a double-check and review the content of what it has provided you with.

Video, Image, and Audio Creation

If you have ever seen a "deep-fake" image, then you know what I am talking about. AI has been able to generate images of what seem like real people based on drawings and by mixing the characteristics of people they identify in images. Similar to this, it can also mimic lip and body movement to create videos or create voices that can be used in audios. Technology has come a long way and today, some creations are so perfect that it is impossible to determine if what we are seeing is reality or not.

This tool, although it can be useful for companies who want to create marketing videos and propaganda, for example, can also pose a threat because of the similarity that it has to what content using "real" people would look like. This could lead to image and voice rights claims and other legal problems. In some cases, people have used Gen-AI to create models and "perfect humans" with perfect features, making it difficult to differentiate what is fake from reality.

Music

In a similar approach used by generative art, AI can create original music and beats that might become your next favorite tune! As you have seen in an example earlier in this book, it is possible to prompt tools such as ChatGPT to create an original song and the tune it should be sung to. The use of Gen-AI in music can be profitable for several companies and artists, who can claim originality of their music because it is based on AI.

However, we must still consider the copyright issues and the use of digital voices that can mimic the voices of humans. Much like with art, there is some controversy in the industry regarding the use of AI to generate chords and beats to songs that would usually be credited to a human. In addition to this, it also begs the question: If an artist uses AI to generate a song, does this mean it is theirs? Or does it belong to the owner of the AI tool? While there is no concrete answer to this question as of yet, we still remain to see what will be decided to regain property rights of these compositions.

Gaming

In gaming, Gen-AI is already in full use. This means enabling the players to access new levels of a certain game as they progress—even if these new levels do not exist! Based on the player performance, preferences, and the game characteristics, it is possible to see new stages of the games being developed and offering the users a personalized approach of the level and the experience.

Software Development

If you have ever dreamed about creating your own program or game, then it is possible to do so with Gen-AI. With its ability to create and complete code, these tools can help users create their own programs in any language they desire. In addition to this, the code will mostly be bug-free (there is no such thing as a software 100% bug free), reducing the time and efforts used to develop software. In addition to this, software developers can use Gen-AI to complete and check their code and see if there are any mistakes, optimizing the creation process.

Healthcare

One of the places that Gen-AI is proving to be the most helpful is in healthcare and medicine. Doctors are using the technology to carry out deeper analysis of patient's clinical conditions, such as identifying cancer cells before they can be seen in traditional tests. In the future, we might see AI creating 3D images with clarity that will give doctors the ability to evaluate their patients with more precision.

Furthermore, the use of Gen-AI is being widely applied in pharmaceutical research. Scientists are using these tools to identify potential new medication and vaccines to combat diseases. It is safe to say that as technology evolves, it is likely we will also see advances in the medical field, increasing positive outcomes and reducing potential human errors.

Entertainment

Similar to what we have seen for AI creating marketing videos and audios, the same can be said for creating entertainment channels for users. If you consider that AI is capable of developing an original story on its own as well as make videos and audios based on the information it is fed, you will also deduce that this can lead to the creation of entertainment material such as animated cartoons. Sounds strange, right?

In addition to this, we have already seen its impact in music, art, and other entertainment areas, such as games. But maybe we don't even need to go that far if we consider that you can actually **play games** with AI tools, as I have shown you. This might be a way to pass time and entertain yourself in a simple manner, such as playing hangman with ChatGPT.

Travel and Tourism

Have you ever imagined having the ability to have a personalized travel guide for your next trip? If not, then you will soon be able to do so because of Gen-AI. One of the many possibilities it will offer in the future is the possibility of creating a specific route based on your interests and preferences. This means giving you the best options of places to visit, where to eat, and even a budget estimate! The perfect trip just a few keyboard strokes away!

Logistics

Have you ever wondered how companies like Uber determine the fee that will be charged based on their dynamic pricing? If you haven't let me tell you that one of the tools that are used to determine this is Gen-AI. The rates charged to the customer is based on the traffic, driver availability, and user demand. This means that the system learns and adapts as the situation changes, a clear sign that this type of technology is being used.

Furthermore, we can consider other tools such as GPS that update traffic conditions in real time another form of Gen-AI, since these are also modified according to the analysis that is performed by the AI algorithm. Therefore, I could say that you are already using this technology and might not even know it! Well, now you do and can see the advantages of embedding this system in traffic monitoring and determining time estimates.

Finance

Gen-AI has been used in finance for some time, to help prevent fraud and protect their users. The technology uses machine learning and pattern analysis to evaluate if there are any compliance issues and carry out the financial analysis of a client's profile. In this regard, some entities are using Gen-AI to establish client profiles for indicating the best way to make their investments based on their investments and portfolio.

Education

Imagine having a study plan that is designed specifically for your needs. This is possible with Gen-AI. By giving it the information that you need and letting it know what are your main difficulties, you can ask the application to generate a specific approach that will focus especially on your needs. This can also be used to create courses by schools and universities. The possibilities are numerous and will be able to help students to have better support and information where their main deficiencies are, much like a personal tutor.

Fashion

One thing we can say is that the fashion industry appears to always be in tune with the newest developments in the technological area. This means that designers can use Gen-AI to create new styles and prints for their products, apart from creating innovative pieces that can become market trends. By using artificial intelligence, there can also be a more economic approach in creating sustainable and technological textiles that will not degrade the environment and reduce the number of scraps in the industry.

FINAL CONSIDERATIONS

As you have seen, Gen-AI is already a part of our present—and it has been for some time. For some circumstances, it has made our lives better, for example with the creation of traffic estimates in navigation systems or with the development of new medication that wasn't previously available. On the other hand, the impacts might not be so positive if you consider the use of AI in creating deep fakes and original art forms that we might not know the origin of. This means that not all AI-generated content is bad and that, whether we like it or not, this technology is here to stay.

As we approach the conclusion of the book, I would like to invite you to reflect upon all the impacts that AI will have in our future—in your future. Do you think that it is possible that you will be replaced? Do you think new jobs will be created? While you don't need to answer me now, that is certainly some food for thought. What I can say is that, after reading this book, you certainly have a lot more information to think about and consider the impacts that AI applications such as ChatGPT will have in our lives.

Give Others the Tools They Need to Speak to ChatGPT in a Way It Understands

You now know the full extent to which ChatGPT can aid you in a myriad of daily tasks. You realize that this new language tool can aid you with everything from marketing and sales to customer service, HR, accounting, and finance. Not only that, but it can enhance your personal life and help you create a healthy lifestyle plan.

Head over to Amazon and let other business people discover how to tap into the full capabilities of ChatGPT. Just one or two sentences could lead them to discover that this technology can help them from Day One—even if they have never used AI, and even if they have never taken part in coding or programming before.

WANT TO HELP OTHERS?

Thank you for helping me on my quest to help business people maximize profits and boost time efficiency. With your aid, other readers can use ChatGPT daily to automate a host of processes, so they can have more free time for more important tasks such as liaising with clients and providing the human touch that consumers still crave.

Scan the QR code to leave a review!

CONCLUSION

Well, this has been a ride! If you were unfamiliar with ChatGPT, I am sure that now you have all the information that you will need to make informed decisions about the chatbot. And what is better: you already have a better grasp about AI technology in general and the way it is changing things in our everyday lives. With all you have seen and the major corporations investing in AI development, it's only a matter of time before the next ChatGPT-like AI tool comes out and takes the world by surprise.

Nevertheless, in the meantime, while the next technological sensation arrives in the market, you have all the tools needed to start using ChatGPT in your business and in your personal life as well. One of the things that you have learned by reading this book—and one of the most important—is how to use the Business Brain Method. If you remember us talking about it back in Chapter 4, it is possible to "train" ChatGPT so that it will give you the desired input to apply to your business.

It does not matter if it is a business that already exists or one that you are creating: The AI application is possible to generate quality content based on the information you feed it and the way you request it to give you information. As you have seen throughout the chapters and the examples they contained, it is essential not only that you are sure about the information you are receiving, but that you know how to correctly prompt the chatbot so that it is the most accurate possible.

If you are working on your existing business, remember to provide ChatGPT with all the relevant information, while taking the necessary precautions regarding any confidential information or trade secrets. If you are starting a new endeavor, keep in mind that you will have limited information since the tool is updated up to 2021, and you might need to provide it with context so that the outcome is more reliable. In any of the cases, you can be sure that the application will be able to help you at least in brainstorming ideas and finding solutions to any challenges you might face business-wise.

At the same time, you have also seen that you can incorporate ChatGPT in several areas of your personal life. It will help you with your writing, dating advice, studies, recipes, and so much more! It all is a matter of how you use it—remember to be cautious and never to use it for medical advice!

Finally, as you have seen in the last chapter, for the time being it seems as if we are not going to be replaced by AI so soon. Even though you saw in the beginning of the book that people are alarmed and jobs are being lost, this only means that we will need to learn and adapt. AI language tools are good at mimicking us, but they still aren't us, which means they lack emotions and critical sense to elaborate thoughts and make decisions. At the end of the day, even though professionals can choose to incorporate ChatGPT in the most varied areas of their business, a human will still be needed to carry out the principal tasks and guide it toward the path it should take.

It is likely, though, that as the use of the application increases, that it will become essential to know how to manage it, and this is where you are already one step ahead. My suggestion, once you close this book, is that you enter the ChatGPT's page and explore even further what it can do for you. Install some of the plugins I have showed you and see how it can integrate with different platforms. May I suggest that you start applying it with friends, since if there is any mistake, it will be less likely it will bring you problems.

Furthermore, once you have fed and trained the brain, it will be time to unleash it, which is when the magic will happen. Providing it with useful prompts will help you discover its full potential—or at least understand what this version can do. If you are willing to wait and pay for the service, I encourage you to try out ChatGPT4 or even enter the search engine Bing to see it in action. By doing this, you will start finding ways to integrate ChatGPT and AI into your business. And do it before you get left behind!

For now, all that is left is for me to wish you success when using the tool! Feel free to come back anytime to this book and use it as a reference guide to understand better how to prompt ChatGPT and look at some suggestions. If you liked the book and feel that it will be helpful for others, I invite you to leave a review and let others know how they will be able to benefit from what you have just read. Good luck with your endeavors and see you soon!

REFERENCES

Abidi, Y. (2023, March 15). *The 5 best new GPT-4 features explained.*
Make Use Of. https://www.makeuseof.com/best-new-gpt4-
features-explained/

Administrator. (2023, January 11). *What is GPT or generative pre-trained
transformer?* Western Balkans Innovation and Research Platform.
https://balkaninnovation.com/what-is-gpt-or-generative-pre-
trained-transformer/

Alston, E. (2023, March 23). *New! Announcing Zapier's ChatGPT plugin.*
Zapier. https://zapier.com/blog/announcing-zapier-chatgpt-
plugin/

Athanasiou, C. (2023, March 15). *Mark Zuckerberg abandons Metaverse
for AI.* Geek Reporter. https://greekreporter.com/2023/03/15/
mark-zuckerberg-abandons-metaverse-ai/

Baraniuk, C. (2017, August 1). *The "creepy Facebook AI" story that captivated the media.* BBC News. https://www.bbc.com/news/technol
ogy-40790258

Browne, R. (2023, April 17). *All you need to know about ChatGPT, the A.I.
chatbot that's got the world talking and tech giants clashing.* CNBC.
https://www.cnbc.com/2023/02/08/what-is-chatgpt-viral-ai-chat
bot-at-heart-of-microsoft-google-fight.html

Chadwick, J. (2022, August 10). *Meta's new AI chatbot BlenderBot 3 calls
Mark Zuckerberg "creepy."* Mail Online. https://www.dailymail.co.
uk/sciencetech/article-11098479/Metas-new-AI-chatbot-
BlenderBot-3-calls-Mark-Zuckerberg-creepy.html

Charles J. C. (2022, August 12). *Meta Facebook Blenderbot AI testdrive.*
LinkedIn. https://www.linkedin.com/pulse/meta-facebook-
blenderbot-ai-testdrive-charles-j-cohen/?trk=pulse-article_more-
articles_related-content-card

ChatGPT integrations in 2023. (2023). Slashdot. https://slashdot.org/soft
ware/p/ChatGPT/integrations

Cheguri, P. (2023, February 2). *Open AI introduces a new AI tool to detect content generated by ChatGPT*. Analytics Insight. https://www.analyt icsinsight.net/open-ai-introduces-a-new-ai-tool-to-detect-content-generated-by-chatgpt/

Chow, A., & Perrigo, B. (2023, February 17). *The AI arms race is on. Start worrying*. Time. https://time.com/6255952/ai-impact-chatgpt-microsoft-google/

DeGeurin, M. (2022, August 6). *Meta's new AI chatbot loves anti-racism and "Mean Girls."* Gizmodo. https://gizmodo.com/meta-facebook-new-ai-chatbot-blenderbot-racism-misinfo-1849378666

Dilmegani, C. (2023, April 17). *Top 70+ generative AI applications / Use cases in 2023*. AI Multiple. https://research.aimultiple.com/genera tive-ai-applications/

Drinkwater, P. (2022, December 30). *7 practical ways to use Chat GPT in your business*. Phil Drinkwater Coach. https://phildrinkwater. coach/7-practical-ways-to-use-chat-gpt-in-your-business/

Duboust, O., & Bello, C. (2023, January 28). *Students are using ChatGPT to do their homework. Should schools ban AI tools, or embrace them?* Euronews. https://www.euronews.com/next/2023/01/28/students-are-using-chatgpt-to-do-their-homework-should-schools-ban-ai-tools-or-embrace-the

Duggal, N. (2023, April 20). *Advantages and disadvantages of Artificial Intelligence*. Simplilearn. https://www.simplilearn.com/advantages-and-disadvantages-of-artificial-intelligence-article

Edwards, J. (2023, February 22). *8 ways to put ChatGPT to work for your business*. InformationWeek. https://www.informationweek.com/big-data/8-ways-to-put-chatgpt-to-work-for-your-business

Elgan, M. (2023, February 1). *6 surprising facts about ChatGPT nobody told you*. Computerworld. https://www.computerworld.com/article/3686616/6-surprising-facts-about-chatgpt-nobody-told-you.html

Eliaçik, E. (2022, May 9). *AI's invisible hand in everyday life*. Dataconomy. https://dataconomy.com/blog/2022/05/09/artificial-intelligence-in-everyday-life/

Eliaçik, E. (2023, February 24). *What is generative AI: Tools, images, and*

more examples. DataConomy. https://dataconomy.com/2023/02/
17/what-is-generative-ai-tools-images/

Elias, J. (2023, February 1). *Google is asking employees to test potential
ChatGPT competitors, including a chatbot called "Apprentice Bard."*
CNBC. https://www.cnbc.com/2023/01/31/google-testing-chat
gpt-like-chatbot-apprentice-bard-with-employees.html

Emilio, N. (n.d.). *The new capabilities of Chat GPT-4 and how to take
advantage of them*. BiSmart. https://blog.bismart.com/en/chat-gpt-
4-new-capabilities

Emily. (2023, January 24). *5 ways you can use Chat GPT to save time and
increase your productivity*. Frappes and Fiction. https://frappesandfic
tion.com/2023/01/24/chat-gpt-productivity/

Entrepreneur Staff. (2023, February 16). *ChatGPT: What is it and how
does it work?* Entrepreneur. https://www.entrepreneur.com/
science-technology/chatgpt-what-is-it-and-how-does-it-work/
445014

Evans, L. (2023, January 12). *Supercharge your ChatGPT prompts (do this)*
[Video]. YouTube. https://www.youtube.com/watch?v=vBREx
D5A5-E&t=204s

Fedyk, Y. (2023, February 15). *7 practical ways to use Chat GPT in your
business*. Inverita. https://inveritasoft.com/article-practical-ways-
to-use-chat-gpt-in-your-business

Gabe A. (2023, April 4). *How to integrate ChatGPT with any app you want!*
Medium. https://levelup.gitconnected.com/heres-a-list-of-some-
popular-apps-that-can-be-integrated-with-chatgpt-ebaea2e91814

Gadgets Now Bureau. (2023, March 17). *Here are the companies using
ChatGPT*. Gadgets Now. https://www.gadgetsnow.com/
slideshows/here-are-the-companies-using-chatgpt/photolist/
98735402.cms?picid=98735411

Gal, U. (2023, February 9). *ChatGPT is a data privacy nightmare. If you've
ever posted online, you ought to be concerned*. The Conversation.
https://theconversation.com/chatgpt-is-a-data-privacy-nightmare-
if-youve-ever-posted-online-you-ought-to-be-concerned-199283

Gindham, A. (2023a, February 20). *20 best ChatGPT use cases to grow your businesses in 2023*. The Writesonic Blog. https://writesonic. com/blog/chatgpt-use-cases/#how-to-use-chatgpt

Gindham, A. (2023b, March 2). *15 best ChatGPT Chrome extensions you must know in 2023*. The Writesonic Blog. https://writesonic.com/ blog/chatgpt-chrome-extensions/

Gupta, A. (2023a, March 23). *Is ChatGPT getting used for office work? New study makes this revelation*. Mint. https://www.livemint.com/news/ india/is-chatgpt-getting-used-for-office-work-new-study-makes-this-revelation-11679552025601.html

Gupta, V. K. (2023b, May 1). *Why AI will never replace humans?* . Antino Labs. https://www.antino.com/blog/why-ai-never-replace-humans/

Hafeez, B. (2022, December 9). *Simple ways GPT-3 ChatBot can make your life easier*. Macro Hive. https://macrohive.com/hive-exclu sives/how-chatgpt-will-change-your-life/

Hern, A. (2022, August 10). *TechScape: Meta's BlenderBot 3 wants to chat – but can you trust it?* The Guardian. https://www.theguardian.com/ technology/2022/aug/10/meta-ai-facebook-blenderbot-3-chatbot

Houghton, B. (2023, February 14). *We asked ChatGPT for dating advice & it was freakishly good* [Video]. Narcity. https://www.narcity.com/ toronto/we-asked-chatgpt-for-dating-advice-it-was-freakishly-good-video

I.Q. Motion. (2021, August 3). *Artificial intelligence in daily life with examples*. Medium. https://becominghuman.ai/artificial-intelli gence-in-daily-life-with-examples-a363502086ff

Ivancie, M. (2023, March 17). *Can OpenAI keep its lead in the AI arms race?* UpMarket. https://www.upmarket.co/blog/can-openai-keep-its-lead-in-the-artificial-intelligence-arms-race/

Jackson, S. (2023, March 21). *Nearly 70% of people using ChatGPT at work haven't told their bosses about it, survey finds*. Business Insider. https:// www.businessinsider.com/70-of-people-using-chatgpt-at-work-havent-told-bosses-2023-3

Jimenez, K. (2023, February 2). "This shouldn't be a surprise" The education community shares mixed reactions to ChatGPT. *USA Today*. https://eu.usatoday.com/story/news/education/2023/01/

30/chatgpt-going-banned-teachers-sound-alarm-new-ai-tech/
11069593002/

Jones, J. (2023, April 3). *AI could automate 25% of all jobs. Here's which are most (and least) at risk.* ZDNET. https://www.zdnet.com/article/ai-could-automate-25-of-all-jobs-heres-which-are-most-and-least-at-risk/

Kashyap, D. (2023, March 25). *Top 5 amazing features of GPT-4 that surpass ChatGPT.* Medium. https://levelup.gitconnected.com/top-5-amazing-features-of-gpt-4-that-surpass-chatgpt-dfedde0e8da1

Kelly, S. M. (2023, March 16). *5 jaw-dropping things GPT-4 can do that ChatGPT couldn't.* CNN Business. https://edition.cnn.com/2023/03/16/tech/gpt-4-use-cases/index.html

Kerridge Commercial Systems. (n.d.). *10 inspirational tech quotes.* https://blog.kerridgecs.com/10-inspirational-tech-quotes

Kharpal, A. (2017, November 6). *Stephen Hawking says A.I. could be "worst event in the history of our civilization."* CNBC. https://www.cnbc.com/2017/11/06/stephen-hawking-ai-could-be-worst-event-in-civilization.html

Kharpal, A. (2023, April 26). *Google had a "Kodak moment" last year as Microsoft takes lead in AI, strategist says.* CNBC. https://www.cnbc.com/2023/04/26/google-had-a-kodak-moment-as-microsoft-takes-lead-in-ai-strategist.html

Kucera, R. (2017, August 7). *The truth behind Facebook AI inventing a new language.* Medium. https://towardsdatascience.com/the-truth-behind-facebook-ai-inventing-a-new-language-37c5d680e5a7

The Learning Network. (2023, February 2). What students are saying about ChatGPT. *The New York Times.* https://www.nytimes.com/2023/02/02/learning/students-chatgpt.html

Leffer, L. (2023, March 16). *Zuckerberg pivots to AI after pivoting to the metaverse.* Gizmodo. https://gizmodo.com/instagram-facebook-mark-zuckerberg-whatsapp-ai-1850232199

Leong, A., & Martindale, J. (2023, April 6). *Google Bard vs. ChatGPT: Which is the better AI chatbot?* Digital Trends. https://www.digitaltrends.com/computing/google-bard-vs-chatgpt-which-is-the-better-ai-chatbot/

Lowe, R., & Leike, J. (2022, January 27). *Aligning language models to follow instructions.* OpenAI. https://openai.com/research/instruction-following

Marr, B. (2023, February 13). *What does ChatGPT really mean for your job?* Forbes. https://www.forbes.com/sites/bernardmarr/2023/02/13/what-does-chatgpt-really-mean-for-your-job/?sh=494ed26b5bda

Mathur, C. (2023, February 2). *Google's Apprentice Bard chatbot could change search forever.* Android Police. https://www.androidpolice.com/google-apprentice-bard-chatgpt/

Medha. (2023, January 4). *10 generative AI use cases that will change how you work.* Fireflies. https://fireflies.ai/blog/generative-ai-use-cases

Mehdi, Y. (2023, February 7). *Reinventing search with a new AI-powered Microsoft Bing and Edge, your copilot for the web.* The Official Microsoft Blog. https://blogs.microsoft.com/blog/2023/02/07/reinventing-search-with-a-new-ai-powered-microsoft-bing-and-edge-your-copilot-for-the-web/

Mihajlovic, I. (2019, June 13). *How artificial intelligence is impacting our everyday lives.* Medium. https://towardsdatascience.com/how-artificial-intelligence-is-impacting-our-everyday-lives-eae3b63379e1

MrNewq. (2023, February 10). *ChatGPT prompt engineering, "Let's think step by step", and other magic phrases.* Medium. https://ai.plainenglish.io/chatgpt-prompt-engineering-lets-think-step-by-step-and-other-magic-phrases-f5c6e143a82a

Nduka, C. (2023, January 17). *Tech giants are in a race to dominate the AI frontier.* HackerNoon. https://hackernoon.com/tech-giants-are-in-a-race-to-dominate-the-ai-frontier

Nicastro, D. (2023, March 1). *ChatGPT is coming for your jobs—and already has succeeded.* CMSWire. https://www.cmswire.com/customer-experience/chatgpt-is-already-replacing-humans-in-the-workplace/

ODSC-Open Data Science. (2023, February 9). *OpenAI releases AI detection to curb ChatGPT abuse.* Medium. https://odsc.medium.com/openai-releases-ai-detection-tool-to-curb-chatgpt-abuse-8d5888ec3877

Oluwaniyi, R. (2023, March 15). *7 reasons why artificial intelligence can't replace humans at work.* Make Use Of. https://www.makeuseof.com/reasons-artificial-intelligence-cant-replace-humans/

OpenAI Editor. (n.d.). *Speech to text.* OpenAI Platform. https://platform.openai.com/docs/guides/speech-to-text/supported-languages

Partida, D. (2023, March 15). *Useful applications of generative AI.* HackerNoon. https://hackernoon.com/useful-applications-of-generative-ai

Phillips, G. (2023, January 31). *OpenAI launches an AI detector tool to counter ChatGPT-generated text. Make Use Of.* https://www.makeuseof.com/openai-launches-ai-detector-counter-chatgpt/

Piper, K. (2022, August 21). *Why is Meta's new AI chatbot so bad?* Vox. https://www.vox.com/future-perfect/23307252/meta-facebook-bad-ai-chatbot-blenderbot

Q.ai. (2023, January 27). *Microsoft confirms its $10 billion investment into ChatGPT, changing how Microsoft competes with Google, Apple and other tech giants.* Forbes. https://www.forbes.com/sites/qai/2023/01/27/microsoft-confirms-its-10-billion-investment-into-chatgpt-changing-how-microsoft-competes-with-google-apple-and-other-tech-giants/?sh=64dbb0b43624

Ruby, M. (2023, January 30). *How ChatGPT works: The models behind the bot.* Medium. https://towardsdatascience.com/how-chatgpt-works-the-models-behind-the-bot-1ce5fca96286

Sha, A. (2023, April 29). *18 examples of AI you're using in daily life in 2023.* Beebom. https://beebom.com/examples-of-artificial-intelligence/

Sharma, M. (2023, January 27). *After job cuts, BuzzFeed employs ChatGPT to create website content.* WION. https://www.wionews.com/technology/after-job-cuts-buzzfeed-employs-chatgpt-to-create-website-content-556395

Sharma, U. (2023, April 21). *10 best ChatGPT Chrome extensions you need to check out.* Beebom. https://beebom.com/best-chatgpt-chrome-extensions/

Shen, M. (2023, March 16). *Top 10 best ChatGPT-based chrome extensions in 2023.* Awesome Screenshot. https://www.awesomescreenshot.com/blog/knowledge/chatgpt-chrome-extension

Shenwai, T. (2023, January 20). *What is generative AI? Concept and applications explained*. MarkTechPost. https://www.marktechpost.com/2023/01/20/what-is-generative-ai-concept-and-applications-explained/

Shukla, R. (2023, February 7). *What is ChatGPT? Can the AI chatbot replace Google in near future - Explained*. Zee Business. https://www.zeebiz.com/technology/news-what-is-chatgpt-founder-name-sam-altman-openai-can-artificial-intelligence-chatbot-replace-google-in-near-future-explained-220988

Slater, D. (2023, February 2). *How to write better prompts for Chat GPT*. GripRoom. https://www.griproom.com/fun/how-to-write-better-prompts-for-chat-gpt

Takyar, A. (2023, January 31). *Generative AI use cases and applications*. LeewayHertz. https://www.leewayhertz.com/generative-ai-use-cases-and-applications/

Teja, R. (2023, February 14). *25 things you can do with ChatGPT*. TechWiser. https://techwiser.com/things-you-can-do-with-chatgpt/

Tellez, A. (2023, March 3). *These major companies are all using ChatGPT - here's why*. Forbes Australia. https://www.forbes.com.au/news/innovation/these-major-companies-are-all-using-chatgpt-heres-why/

Timothy, M. (2022, December 20). *11 things you can do with ChatGPT*. MUO. https://www.makeuseof.com/things-you-can-do-with-chatgpt/

Truly, A. (2023, April 6). *GPT-4: How to use, new features, availability, and more*. Digital Trends. https://www.digitaltrends.com/computing/chatgpt-4-everything-we-know-so-far/

University of Maryland School of Medicine. (2023, April 4). *ChatGPT provides correct health advice about 88% of the time, study finds*. News Medical. https://www.news-medical.net/news/20230404/ChatGPT-provides-correct-health-advice-about-8825-of-the-time-study-finds.aspx

Vanian, J. (2022, December 13). *Why tech insiders are so excited about ChatGPT, a chatbot that answers questions and writes essays*. CNBC.

https://www.cnbc.com/2022/12/13/chatgpt-is-a-new-ai-chatbot-that-can-answer-questions-and-write-essays.html

Victor, A. (2021, July 24). *10 uses of artificial intelligence in day to day life.* Daffodil. https://insights.daffodilsw.com/blog/10-uses-of-artificial-intelligence-in-day-to-day-life

Vincent, J. (2023, February 7). *Microsoft announces new Bing and Edge browser powered by upgraded ChatGPT AI.* The Verge. https://www.theverge.com/2023/2/7/23587454/microsoft-bing-edge-chatgpt-ai

West, J. (2023, January 9). *How to train Chat GPT on your business* [Video]. YouTube. https://www.youtube.com/watch?v=P_CHTabYa-0&t=96s

Yalalov, D. (2022, December 23). *5 unexpected ways to use ChatGPT in your Tinder convos and get a date.* Metaverse Post. https://mpost.io/5-unexpected-ways-to-use-chatgpt-in-your-tinder-convos-and-get-a-date/

Yang, S. (2022, December 10). *The abilities and limitations of ChatGPT.* Anaconda. https://www.anaconda.com/blog/the-abilities-and-limitations-of-chatgpt

Young, A. (2023, January 29). Advanced ChatGPT prompt tutorial (10x your productivity with AI) [Video]. YouTube. https://www.youtube.com/watch?v=HGDxu3kPErs&t=115s

Made in the USA
Las Vegas, NV
22 January 2024

84739579R00108